POLICE PUBLIC CALL BOX

POLICE

PUBLIC
CALL

BOX

POLICE TELEPHONE
FREE
FOR USE OF
PUBLIC
ADVICE & ASSISTANCE
OBTAINABLE IMMEDIATELY
OFFICERS & CARS
RESPOND TO ALL CALLS
PULL TO OPEN

BBC

DOCTOR WHO

ROLEPLAYING GAME

ALL OF TIME AND SPACE
VOLUME 1

✺ CREDITS

WRITING: *Ghost Engines* by Gareth Ryder-Hanrahan
Northern Knights by Walt Ciechanowski
Schrödinger's Expedition by Nick Huggins
The Tomb of Cleopatra by Timothy Ferguson
EDITING: Andrew Kenrick
COVER: Paul Bourne
GRAPHIC DESIGN AND LAYOUT: Paul Bourne
CREATIVE DIRECTOR: Jon Hodgson
ART DIRECTOR: Jon Hodgson
PUBLISHER: Dominic McDowall
PROOFREADER: Peter Gilham and Brian Swift.
SPECIAL THANKS: Ross McGlinchey and the BBC
team for all their help.

The **Doctor Who Roleplaying Game** uses the
Vortex system, designed by David F. Chapman.

Published by Cubicle 7 Entertainment Ltd
Suite D3 Unit 4 Gemini House, Hargreaves Road,
Groundwell Industrial Estate, Swindon, SN25 5AZ, UK.
(UK reg. no.6036414).

Find out more about us and our games at
www.cubicle7.co.uk

Printed by: Standartų Spaustuvė
www.standart.lt, Vilnius, Lithuania.

✿ CONTENTS

INTRODUCTION

'SO ALL OF TIME AND ALL OF SPACE IS SITTING OUT THERE. A BIG BLUE BOX.
PLEASE DON'T EVEN ARGUE.'

The Doctor is not a good man. He's not a bad man. He's not a hero. He's definitely not a president nor an officer. What he is is an idiot with a box and a screwdriver. Passing through. Helping out. Learning. He doesn't need an army, because he's got his companions, and together they have the most extraordinary adventures.

All of Time and Space contains four such adventures for the **Doctor Who Roleplaying Game**:

GHOST ENGINES
A prison ship from the far future has crashed in Earth's past and its cargo – a tyrannical psychic vampire named Zoroth, along with a gang of bat-like monsters – has been unwittingly freed beneath Victorian London.

NORTHERN KNIGHTS
Elizabethan England is ravaged by a mysterious plague spread by silver rats – Cybermats! The Cybermen have formed a secret alliance with a rebellious noble and the soul of England and Scotland are at stake!

THE TOMB OF CLEOPATRA
An archaeological dig in modern-day Egypt has uncovered the fabled Tomb of Cleopatra, once thought lost to the sands of time. But if this is an ancient tomb, how come there's the severed head of a Cyberman buried inside it?

SCHRÖDINGER'S EXPEDITION
Orbiting the planet Pilatedes is a vast, abandoned space station known as Anomaly IV. How did it get there and what was it for – and, more importantly, what's inside? Nobody's set foot on it for a long time – until now, when two expeditions from parallel dimensions set out to discover its secrets.

ABOUT THE ADVENTURES
The adventures in this book are all designed to be used with pretty much any group of characters, whether that's the Doctor and Clara, your own Time Lord and their companions, Professor Song and her team or even Kate Stewart and UNIT. They all start in the present day, but from there swiftly head into the past or the future, so assume that your characters at least have access to some means of time travel – so River might have to use that Vortex Manipulator of hers, or Osgood might have to get one of the devices in the Black Archive to work.

GHOST ENGINES

GHOST ENGINES

A prison ship from the far future has crashed into Earth's past and its cargo – a tyrannical psychic vampire named Zoroth, along with a gang of bat-like monsters – has been unwittingly freed beneath Victorian London. The ship's warden and gaoler, a psychic alien named Peqod, managed to survive the crash too and is preventing Zoroth from escaping the past. But Zoroth wants his revenge, and with the help of a Victorian engineer named Sir Arnold Heath is building a gigantic time trap to capture Peqod so that he might return to have his revenge on the future.

Now, the railways of England have been turned to a darker purpose and strange ghost trains stalk the landscape, searching for Peqod. But, as the net closes in and the time trap prepares to spring, unwitting time travellers are ensnared instead...

⚙ ADVENTURE SYNOPSIS

The characters find themselves transported to 1889 after exploring a disused railway tunnel in Marnock in the present day, meeting up with some old Victorian companions who are also investigating strange events on the railways of England. The tunnels seems to be where the trouble started, so the characters start poking around there but while investigating, they're attacked by Kith, and helped

by the Conciliator... and then they see the strangest train imaginable.

That weird train bears the livery of the Great Encompassing Railway, so they will inevitably look into that company's background. One trail of clues leads to the mansion of Sir Arnold Heath, and the secrets concealed in his cellars. Another trail leads to tunnels like the one at Marnock, where there's been a string of mysterious disappearances. Finally, the characters find the secret heart of the Great Encompassing Railway – the Ghost Engine – and meet the escaped prisoner Zoroth, who tries to paint himself as the good guy and his gaoler Peqod as the villain. Whether duped or not, it's all aboard the Hunting Train for a showdown on the tracks!

THREATS

There are longer write-ups of each of these characters later in the scenario, but to summarise:

Zoroth: Megalomaniac alien renegade Conciliator who wants to recapture Peqod and return to wreak havoc in the far future. His ability to time travel was removed as part of his punishment, so he needs to recapture Peqod to return to the distant future. He's pretending to be a good guy and has fooled Sir Arnold.

He possesses the bodies of various train workers to pose as Sir Arnold's business partner.

Sir Arnold Heath: Well-meaning but deluded engineer. He's become rich and powerful thanks to Zoroth's influence, and is convinced that he must catch the 'Monster' that Zoroth seeks to balance the books. Catching the monster will justify his undeserved good fortune. Play him as... well, he's basically Bertie Wooster trying to be Captain Ahab.

The Steamborgs: Former railway workers, soldiers or dockworkers kidnapped by Zoroth and upgraded with cybernetic parts. Some are grateful to Heath for 'healing' them; others work under duress and are virtual prisoners. Zoroth can possess any of them as replacement bodies for himself. The Steamborgs are a secret army – their existence is not common knowledge by any means. Stats for the Steamborgs can be found on pg. 23.

The Kith: Nasty anarchistic space bats living in the tunnels. Stats for the Kith can be found on pg. 12.

The Conciliators: Far-future authoritarian psychic space police. They can travel through space and time, possess victims and generally act like scary space ghosts.

Conciliator Peqod: The Conciliator tasked with bringing Zoroth and the Kith to their exile. He's currently on the run, but unable to escape because Zoroth has turned the railways into a giant trap. He's currently possessing the body of Simon Fitzhugh.

✲ THE GREAT ENCOMPASSING RAILWAYS COMPANY

The "Great Compass" is a new railway company, less than a decade old in 1889, but in those years it has grown at an astounding rate. Its trains are faster than its competitors, and its railways smoother and more direct. The owner and founder of the company is an engineer and newly minted Knight of the Realm named Sir Arnold Heath. The newspapers acclaim him as a genius, one of the architects of the Empire's golden age, the scandal sheets call him the most eligible bachelor in London, and no one – no one who matters, anyway – looks into the strange circumstances of his company or the plight of his workforce.

The clue is in the name of his company. Sir Arnold may bluster that the name speaks of his ambition, "to gird this whole blessed island in a ring of swift railways", but that's not quite it. Ten years ago, Sir

Arnold was just a junior engineer working on a new railway tunnel. The digging team found a strange metal object buried in the Sussex hillside. That broken thing – the crashed remains of a prison ship – was the foundation of Heath's success.

Zoom out. Millions of years in the future, the Constant of Harmony rules a thousand star systems. It's a glorious star empire, home to hundreds of different races including trillions of humans. Conciliators enforce peace and justice within the Constant of Harmony. These psychic entities are the mailed fist of Harmony. They can phase in and out of the Time Vortex, appearing when and where they are needed to protect Harmony. They possess any convenient bodies, turning them into enforcers of justice. The Constant does not kill unnecessarily, though. Dissidents and criminals are punished by temporal exile. The Conciliators capture these criminals and bring them back in time to the distant past of the universe, exiling them on deserted worlds.

One such ship carried a prisoner called Zoroth. By the standards of the Constant of Harmony, Zoroth was a monster and a deviant, determined to wreak anarchy and suffering across the stars. Zoroth was a renegade Conciliator, a psychic monster capable of leaping from host to host. His escort on this voyage to exile was the Conciliator who captured him: Conciliator Peqod.

Their ship crashed on Earth. Peqod ejected before it landed, taking with him the control console for the ship. He intended to signal for help, but before the Conciliator could make contact with the far future, Heath's engineers freed Zoroth from the prison ship.

Zoroth wants revenge on the Constant of Harmony, but for that he needs a time machine. He built the Great Encompassing Railway to capture the Conciliator. The engines and the railway tracks are components of a vast machine that stops the Conciliator from escaping. To convince Heath to

GHOST ENGINES

help him, Zoroth lied and claimed that the Conciliator was actually the prisoner, while Zoroth himself was the gaoler.

Now, using Heath as his agent, Zoroth has established an extradimensional base under London, staffed by kidnapped prisoners. His goal is to find the Conciliator and get the control codes for the Conciliator Ship. He has 'Hunting Trains' staffed by steam-powered cyborgs that wander the tunnels, looking for the missing Conciliator.

Also on board the ship was a gang of vicious monsters, the Kith. They escaped into the countryside, and now hunt the Conciliator too.

⚙ 1. ARRIVAL

The adventure opens in the modern day. The characters have learnt that people – children, mainly – are going missing near an old railway tunnel. Tragic, yes, but not normally the concern of time travellers, UNIT, Torchwood or whoever they might be. Except that a witness reported a young boy named Simon vanishing into thin air. Suitably intrigued, the characters arrive at the old Marnock Spur tunnel to investigate. It's an old disused Victorian railway tunnel that runs through a hillside; the old bricks are marked with graffiti and stained by soot. Looking around, there's no sign of anything unusual. If a character scans using an appropriate Gadget, then an Ingenuity + Technology

roll (Difficulty 9) picks up the following (you can also use this as an opportunity to explain the basic die mechanic if you're using this adventure as an introduction to the game).

* There's a lingering energy signature in the rails here.
* There's some sort of circuitry in the brickwork. Very old, very advanced...

...and then there's a flare of blue light, and a ghostly wind howls down the tunnel, as the Ghost Engines thunder into life. The characters fall unconscious as they're dragged back in time.

FOUND BY FRIENDS

Switch to Victorian England, where you have the perfect opportunity to introduce characters from that era into your game – Jenny, Strax and Madame Vastra, Jago and Litefoot, even Jackson Lake and Rosita – either played by the other players or as NPCs. For the purposes of the rest of this adventure, we'll assume they're the Paternoster Gang. They've been hired to investigate a monster sighting in the underground – some sort of monstrous bat-like thing attacked a passenger train, and the police are baffled. They just picked up a burst of temporal radiation. Following the energy leads them to a construction site owned by the Great Encompassing Company, where they find the unconscious forms of the time travellers. Hopefully, they recognise at least one of the characters.

As Vastra, Jenny and Strax approach, they see a small glowing humanoid figure vanish into thin air. This was the Conciliator in the body of Simon, who moved the Doctor and the other travellers away from the tunnel where they arrived, in case the Kith got them while they were unconscious.

The Paternoster Gang will suggest that it's probably best to get the time travellers to safety where they can recover (time travel without a capsule *hurts*). Vastra's home isn't far away by carriage.

The adventure proper begins with the time-shifted characters waking up at at 13 Paternoster Row . The characters have no idea how they got here – the last thing any of them remember is walking through the tunnel.

Looking outside, the characters can tell they're in 19th century London – some of them might even have been here before. Give the characters a chance to introduce themselves and compare notes.

VICTORIAN LONDON

Take a moment to describe the sights and sounds of Victorian London. It's 1889 – Queen Victoria's on the throne, Robert Cecil's the Prime Minister, the British army is fighting a war in the Sudan, and there's a big strike on the docks, which in September will be a victory for the unions when the dockers' pay is increased.

Steam trains thunder through the capital, but the characters will probably get from place to place by walking or by hiring a horse-drawn hackney cab – or by the London Underground, which by 1889 had more than forty stations along several unconnected lines, with trains drawn by smaller steam locomotives.

Madame Vastra has a large wardrobe of clothes and is quite wealthy, so the characters can outfit themselves in period clothing (top hats are cool).

⚙ 2. INVESTIGATING THE RAILWAY

Everything seems to point to the railway tunnels. The characters can either head back to Marnock, or the tunnels near where they were found, or the tunnel where the bat-like monster was seen – they're all different places, but they each lead to the same scene.The characters leave the hustle and bustle of the busy London streets behind them, and head into the tunnels.

Exploring the dark tunnels, they encounter a one-armed watchman named Bert. He toddles into view with his flickering lantern held high. The characters can either sneak past Bert (Coordination + Subterfuge, Difficulty 9) or talk to him (Presence + Convince to get him talking, Difficulty of between 9 and 15 depending on roleplaying).

BERT THE WATCHMAN

Playing Bert:

- You're a former railway engineer, but you lost your arm when a boiler exploded. Now, you patrol the tunnels, to stop vagrants and thieves from getting in.
- You've seen strange things down here, but that might be a combination of smoke inhalation and gin. If they weren't hallucinations, they were ghostly trains made of blue fire, with the grim faces of the dead staring out of the windows, or tremendous black bats with glowing eyes, or little men who laugh and call him names. Bert's something of an unreliable witness – the first two are genuine encounters with the Hunting Train and the Kith, but the last one is mostly whiskey.
- You're smarter than you seem, when you're not sozzled.
- Fold one arm behind your back when playing Bert.

Questioning Bert:

- No one's allowed down here! It's dangerous. You could get run over by a train in the dark.
- The trains aren't the only danger. Thieves and gypsies and foreigners and... other things.
- Bert works for the Great Encompassing Railway. They're a new company, bound for great things. He's a huge admirer of Mr Heath, the founder of the company. He's an engineer to recall the works of Brunel or Stephenson. Charitable, too – why, he holds dinners for those injured and maimed through their work!

ALIEN TECH

Once the characters get past Bert, or convince him to show them where he saw the strange things, they end up in a tunnel like the one at Marnock in the 21st century. There's a 30-foot-long section of tunnel wall that was recently recovered in new brickwork, with the logo of the Encompassing Railway emblazoned upon it. Looking around, there's a second stretch of identical brickwork another 200 feet down the tracks.

Scanning (with a Sonic Screwdriver or some other home-made Gadget) reveals the presence of more high-tech circuitry behind the bricks. Removing the bricks reveals the circuits. Examining them reveals:

- They're *very* advanced technology. Well, actually, they're a really low-tech example of very advanced technology. Looks like someone got stranded here in this barbaric wilderness and strung together a telephone out of tin cans and string. Or, more accurately, a Dimensional Shunt out of iron and bronze.
- It's a Dimensional Shunt. On its own, it does nothing, but if you were standing here when a burst of Hyperyon particles passed through, then whomp! Boom! You'd be shunted. It could teleport you in space or time, or even sideways into a pocket dimension. Or, you know, disintegrate you. It all depends on the particle's energy level when it hits the shunt.
- That could have been what happened to Simon. Well, hopefully not the disintegration part.
- You need a lot of power to generate Hyperyon particles. It's not easy at all.

THE THIEF AND THE RUNAWAY

While the science-y characters examine the circuits, call for Awareness + Subterfuge rolls (Difficulty 15) from the disinterested characters. Those who succeed spot a shadowy figure moving in the, er, shadows. Investigating, they find a genuine Victorian grubby street urchin hiding in a niche. Calming her down (Presence + Convince, Difficulty 12) gets the characters a garbled version of her story.

- Her name's Mary. She's 13 years old. She came down here with Mr Rook to pick pockets on the trains, but she ran away. She's scared of Rook.
- She got lost in the darkness. She was all alone, scared and desperate, and then this boy took her hand and told her to run. He brought her to this tunnel and told her to go this way. (This was Simon/Peqod).
- There are things down in these tunnels, terrible things. They're hungry.
- Mr Rook's chasing her. He's coming. Please, help her!

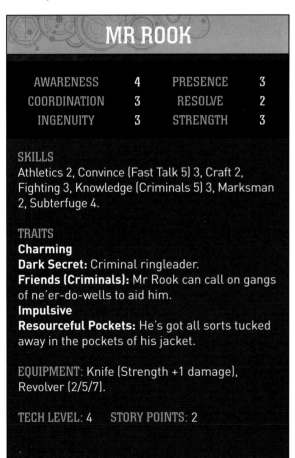

MR ROOK

AWARENESS	4	PRESENCE	3
COORDINATION	3	RESOLVE	2
INGENUITY	3	STRENGTH	3

SKILLS
Athletics 2, Convince (Fast Talk 5) 3, Craft 2, Fighting 3, Knowledge (Criminals 5) 3, Marksman 2, Subterfuge 4.

TRAITS
Charming
Dark Secret: Criminal ringleader.
Friends (Criminals): Mr Rook can call on gangs of ne'er-do-wells to aid him.
Impulsive
Resourceful Pockets: He's got all sorts tucked away in the pockets of his jacket.

EQUIPMENT: Knife (Strength +1 damage), Revolver (2/5/7).

TECH LEVEL: 4   **STORY POINTS:** 2

A moment later, the characters see a lamp bobbling along the tunnel as it approaches. It's Mr Rook – he runs a gang of thieves and cutpurses. He's dressed in a threadbare suit, and he's got a small revolver in his hand, which he hides in a pocket as soon as he sees the characters. He then adopts an obsequious tone, begging their pardons and thanking them for finding his wayward daughter. If the characters hand Mary over, then Rook grabs her and marches her down the tunnel. If, as is much more likely, they refuse, then he draws his gun and threatens them.

3. ATTACK OF THE KITH

While the characters are dealing with Mr Rook, the Kith attack. These alien horrors resemble slimy bats with hands for feet, and razor-sharp blades on their wings. They're as intelligent as humans (actually, a bit brighter on average), but they're too chaotic and, well, lazy to form their own civilisation. They exist as parasites and troublemakers on the fringes of more developed civilisations, like the Constant of Harmony. The Kith consider everyone outside their immediate family group to be meat. To the Kith, the characters are lunch. What they really want is to destroy Peqod before he contacts the Conciliators, recaptures them and exiles them somewhere without as much delicious meat.

They're really, really fast and hard to hit, and they can see very well in the darkness. The first Kith attack should be on Mr Rook (assuming the characters haven't already taken him down), so the players get to see how nasty the monsters are.

- It's hard to tell how many Kith there are – assume one per character, but bring in more from the shadows if needed.
- If the characters stay and fight, then bring in the Ghost Train at a suitably dramatic juncture.
- The Kith are photosensitive – a bright light or a loud noise will drive them away
- The easiest way to deal with their fast movement is to make yourself a target – if one character stands in the way of an oncoming Kith and willingly takes the blow, the Kith loses its defensive bonus against attacks from other characters.
- Running's an option – the Kith have Rook to eat, after all.

Ways to make the peril interesting:

- Attack the characters holding the light sources. The only thing worse than being attacked by flying, cackling cannibal bats is being attacked by flying cackling cannibal bats in dark.
- Rook's revolver may be lying on the ground for a character to grab. Ditto crowbars or other

GHOST ENGINES

tools left by the work-crew who installed the brickwork.

- If the characters split up, there are sidings and access tunnels to hide in.
- An underground train might rush by at an inopportune moment.

KITH

AWARENESS	3	PRESENCE	3
COORDINATION	4	RESOLVE	3
INGENUITY	3	STRENGTH	6

They're scary flapping bat-people from the far far future. They're vermin of the spaceways, snacking on low-tech planets.

SKILLS
Athletics 4, Fighting 3, Subterfuge 3, Survival 2.

TRAITS
Alien
Alien Appearance: Look a bit like a bat-person, flap a bit like a bat-person.
Alien Senses (Dark Vision)
Fear Factor (1): The Kith gain a +2 bonus to actively scare or intimidate someone.
Flight (Major)
Natural Weapons – Claws: 3/6/9 damage.
Phobia (Light)
Superfast: The Kith gain a +6 bonus to Coordination + Fighting rolls to dodge attacks if they have space to move.

TECH LEVEL: 4   STORY POINTS: 1

THE GHOST TRAIN

You can bring this in to rescue the characters from the Kith, or as a cryptic encounter after they escape from the bat things.

The brickwork flares blue, just like it did in the tunnel at Marnock, and a train appears on the tracks, rattling at high speed towards the characters. It's a London underground train, but not like any train they've seen before. Electric lights illuminate it, circuits drive it and it's armoured like a tank. Hollow-eyed men stare out through gunports, some wearing suits like deep-sea divers and carrying strange rifles. This is the Hunting Train, which the characters may see a lot more of later on (see **The Hunting Expedition** on page 22).

If the Kith are still nearby, then the men on the train turn the harsh light of an electric searchlight on the bat-things and let off a volley of gunfire at the beasts, sending the Kith squealing into the darkness.

The train rushes down the tunnel to that second stretch of brickwork, which again flares blue, and the train vanishes.

- The characters clearly see the logo of the Encompassing Railway on the train, although it's partially concealed by armour. Maybe the train belonged to the railway before it was "upgraded".
- You might decide to have someone from the train grab an injured Rook, so you can bring him back as a Steamborg later on.
- Anyone making an Awareness + Medicine roll (Difficulty 12) spots that most of the men on the train are maimed in some way. Lots of war wounds, battle scars and the like. Some seem to have mechanical limbs or eyes – way beyond the technology of this era.

- A successful Science + Technology roll (Difficulty 15) lets the players make some guesses about the technology used – the better the success, the closer to being right their guesses will be. The train's an odd mix of 19th century engineering and far-future tech, just like the brickwork. The same hand is behind both, obviously enough. More interestingly, those 'diving suits' that some of the passengers wore were electrically charged, probably on the same frequency as the human neuro-electric system – the sort of thing you'd wear if you were worried about being possessed by a psychic entity.

- If a character tries leaping onboard the train as it passes, that's a Coordination + Athletics roll, Difficulty 21 – nearly impossible! If the player succeeds, then one of the men in the diving suits tries to dislodge the stowaway with a rifle butt, and the player must succeed in a Strength + Resolve test (Difficulty 18) to stay on.
- If by some miracle a character makes it on board, then you've got two choices:
  - If the character is an alien (obviously or not), such as the Doctor or Madame Vastra, then the men on board the train assume that this supernatural being is their quarry, the Monster that Sir Heath seeks. They start firing. If the character stays on the train, they'll be killed.
  - Another character goes with the train into the pocket dimension (see **The Ghost Engine**, pg. 19). The character gets to glimpse the pocket dimension (a realm of gears and factories and steam power, all built around a silvery cylinder suspended in a web of chains) before being knocked unconscious. The character wakes up in London a few hours later, with an invitation to dinner at Sir Heath's mansion that evening. Zoroth wants to ascertain who these new players are before dealing with them.

⚙ OPTIONAL SCENE: INSPECTOR CRANNEL

If you've played through the first few scenes a bit quickly, then you can bring in Inspector Crannel now, as the characters emerge from the tunnels. Crannel's an old enemy of Madame Vastra – when Vastra first awoke, she attacked tunnel workers. The Doctor taught Vastra the error of her ways, but Crannel's always suspected the mysterious Masked Woman had something to do with all those deaths. Even after all these years, he's refused to give up the hunt. He doesn't know *what* Vastra is, but he suspects she isn't human.

Crannel and his police show up as the characters emerge from underground. He challenges Vastra to explain what she and these 'vagabonds' were doing in the area.

He questioned Bert the Watchman, who reported strange events down in the tunnels. Vastra knows all about strange events in the tunnels, doesn't she? He wonders aloud if there'll be more "unexplained deaths", and suggests to Jenny that she should find better employment, as her mistress may lead her into immoral ways.

Crannel may let slip the following:

- A number of people have vanished in the tunnels recently. No one of consequence, and as far as he's concerned it can only be a good thing if a pack of thieves and beggars vanish. Still, they can't have a public panic, not after the whole Ripper fiasco.
- There are stories of a beast or beasts roaming the tunnels. All nonsense, of course.
- The Encompassing Railway Company is holding some sort of dinner soon for unfortunates and orphans. They've even laid on special trains to bring the beggars into central London.

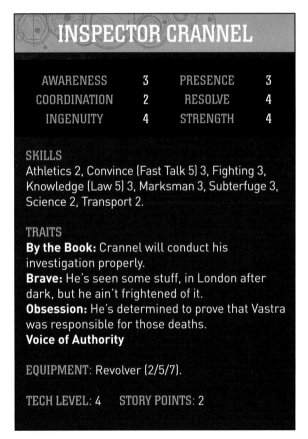

INSPECTOR CRANNEL

AWARENESS	3	PRESENCE	3
COORDINATION	2	RESOLVE	4
INGENUITY	4	STRENGTH	4

SKILLS
Athletics 2, Convince (Fast Talk 5) 3, Fighting 3, Knowledge (Law 5) 3, Marksman 3, Subterfuge 3, Science 2, Transport 2.

TRAITS
By the Book: Crannel will conduct his investigation properly.
Brave: He's seen some stuff, in London after dark, but he ain't frightened of it.
Obsession: He's determined to prove that Vastra was responsible for those deaths.
Voice of Authority

EQUIPMENT: Revolver (2/5/7).

TECH LEVEL: 4   STORY POINTS: 2

⚙ 4. INVESTIGATIONS

The Encompassing Railway company seems to be at the heart of the mystery, and it's connected to those teleporting brickworks. Time to do a little research.

Most of the information here can be easily obtained from newspapers or a cursory investigation. Anything without a Difficulty number in the lists below is common knowledge and doesn't require a roll. If a fact is a little harder to uncover, we've listed the Difficulty to learn it. Let the players decide how they're digging up the info (probably

GHOST ENGINES

Presence + Convince to question people, or Ingenuity + Knowledge to dig through newspaper archives and obscure records).

THE ENCOMPASSING RAILWAY COMPANY

- The Encompassing Railway Company is a relatively new but hugely successful company, founded by Sir Arnold Heath. They made their fortune by introducing a new, more efficient form of locomotive, then started buying up railway lines across the country.
- The company's expanded aggressively. They've got railways across the whole of England, circling the entire island, although most of their lines are centred on London.
- (Difficulty 12) They've got a poor safety record, which may be why Sir Arnold has taken such a public interest in the health of maimed war veterans. His engineering works have taken as many limbs as gangrene and Russian shells did in the Crimea.
- (Difficulty 12) The Encompassing Company's headquarters is a fine building in the middle of London. There's a charitable dinner there tonight; the company's bringing in several train-loads of orphans and maimed veterans, and they'll be wined and dined as though they were gentry for the evening (see **The Stolen Passengers** on pg. 18).

SIR ARNOLD HEATH

- He's somewhat secretive. He comes from a good engineering family, but didn't excel until his mid-twenties.
- He was one of two survivors when a newly dug tunnel collapsed near Marnock ten years ago.
- (Difficulty 12) He went into business with the other survivor, a worker named Hollis. Within two years, Heath was unimaginably wealthy.
- (Difficulty 12) Hollis died a few months after. Since then, Heath's been seen with a succession of mysterious 'business partners', all of whom appear to come from nothing and then vanish again. (Investigation won't reveal this fact, but these 'business partners' are possessed by Zoroth – his hosts burn out after only a few years).
- He's a *very* eligible bachelor. After all, a still-young man in possession of a vast fortune must be in want of a wife.
- He purchased the old Aubreville mansion a few years ago – it's an estate on the edge of London. He receives few visitors there. He's made several alterations to the mansion (see **Heath's Mansion** on pg. 15).

DIMENSIONAL SHUNT SYSTEM

Really, only a Boffin from the future (such as the Doctor, obviously) can work directly on this, although Madame Vastra has some knowledge of high technology – she was in contact with the 51st century Silurians – and Professor Litefoot's seen something similar on his previous adventures.

However, another character can help a Boffin with their work, giving them a +2 bonus if the player can describe a plausible way of helping – taking readings, grabbing samples of brickwork and so on.

- (Difficulty 15) The character recognises this technology. Hyperyon gates? Psychic possession? Dimensional shunts? It's Constant of Harmony technology.
  - The Constant of Harmony is a multi-species empire that arises a few million years in the future. It's... well, it's very safe. Very, very safe. No arguments, no wars, no dissent. They've got these things called Conciliators, who are half police, half time-travelling psychic ghosts that step in and sort out problems.
  - Those shunts need an external power source to activate them. There's no way to make *that* with 19th century technology. It'll be big, though, and require a lot of power.

- It's possible for a Boffin to jury-rig a Gadget to activate the shunts by spending 2 Story Points and making a Jiggery-Pokery roll (Ingenuity + Technology, Difficulty 15). Using such a Gadget, the characters can short-cut to **Scene 7: The Ghost Engine**.

BACK TO THE FUTURE

It's also possible to reactivate the shunt that dragged the characters back to the 19th century. This little temporal sidetrack was caused by Peqod the Conciliator, so it's fading, but the Boffin can boost their Gadget with a third Story Point to visit the 21st century. Travelling back to the future lets the characters pick up some useful equipment (say, the TARDIS) before zooming back to the story.

❀ 5. HEATH'S MANSION

Arnold Heath came from respectable but not especially wealthy middle-class stock, but he purchased a rambling 18th century mansion from a penniless noble family. It's a big, ugly, poorly planned pile of masonry, surrounded by extensive gardens. Sir Arnold's known to be a very private man, and receives few guests at his mansion. Even functions like the upcoming dinner for orphans and unfortunates are held in the Encompassing Railway House in the middle of the city, not out here.

There are two notable features visible from the road. Firstly, there's "Heath's Folly", a railway track that runs through the garden. It's not connected to

anything, and just runs in a ring around the house. He uses it to test engine designs on occasion. If the characters get close enough to examine the rail line, they find that it's got a similar magnetic resonance to the train lines elsewhere, and there's an archway over the track at one point that has the same Dimensional Shunt circuits that the characters found in the rail tunnels under London.

Secondly, there's a new tower built at the back of the house, above his workshop. According to local rumour, this tall tower attracts lightning bolts. Certainly, whenever there's a storm, the tower is wreathed in crackling thunderbolts.

The mansion has a small staff, headed by Heath's valet, the admirable George. Notably, some of the groundkeepers and the workers in the workshop are Zoroth's cybernetic creations.

WALKING IN

Sir Arnold does not normally receive guests. If the characters present themselves at the door, they're met by his valet, George. A gentleman's gentleman, that's our George. Utterly unflappable, and completely discreet. The sort of person in whom you could confide that one's business partner is a body-jumping alien from the distant future, and who would respond with nothing more than an imperceptibly raised eyebrow.

A good story coupled with a Presence + Convince roll (Difficulty 9-18, depending on the story) gets the

characters past George. The players will doubtless come up with some semi-plausible excuse like "we're from the department of train inspections, please look at our Psychic Paper" to "so, Sir Arnold, may I present the very eligible and marriageable Ms Oswald... oh, stay quiet Clara". Alternatively, the characters could just turn up and say "hello, we're time travellers," and George will show them in. Sir Arnold's partner warned him to expect possible intruders.

If the characters get in through the front door (or disguise themselves as servants, or some other ruse), then they end up in either the study or the workshop.

SNEAKING IN

The mansion is guarded. There are several Steamborgs among the groundkeeping staff, and they work both night and day (there's something unwholesome about mowing the lawn at four in the morning...). Sneaking past them requires an Awareness + Subterfuge roll or a clever stratagem.

If the alarm is raised, then the Steamborgs attempt to capture and restrain the characters; prisoners will be brought to the workshop. If they can't capture them, then they raise the alarm, and the Hunting Train appears on the Folly railway. The Steamborgs onboard level weapons at the characters, but won't shoot to kill. The characters can either surrender or flee.

THE STUDY

Heath's study is where he meets his guests. It's a reflection of his insecurity; huge bookcases and gilded chandeliers and paintings by fashionable artists, all say "I am as intelligent and cultured as my reputation holds me to be". It's clear that many of the books have never been opened and few of the paintings have any real artistic merit.

On one wall is a large map of Britain, with the railways owned by the Encompassing Railway Company marked in red. Interestingly, he's deliberately purchased railways to form a complete perimeter around most of the country. From above, it looks oddly like a maze or a net. There are also small red and black flags on the map, all on or near the railways. Most of the black flags (representing sightings of the Kith) are near London. The red flags (representing sightings of Peqod the Conciliator) are all over the map. A successful Awareness + Ingenuity roll (Difficulty 15) or a close examination of the map notes that a flag has been recently added near Marnock.

If the characters meet with Heath, he greets them here (see **Meeting Sir Arnold**, below).

THE WORKSHOP

The workshop at the back of the mansion resembles a stage-set for a performance of *Frankenstein* if you replaced the monster with train parts. Half-assembled engines and models lie about the place, mysterious liquids bubble in jars, and huge crackling coils sizzle with barely-contained energy. Notably, there's a thick web of power cables snaking down from the tower above and running into a trapdoor that goes to the cellars under the house.

Examining the equipment here with Ingenuity + Science, Craft or Technology (Difficulty 9) confirms that it's way beyond the 19th century. A character who has visited that part of the far-future can identify some of the techniques as being reminiscent of the Constant of Harmony.

If the characters get taken prisoner by the Steamborgs, they'll be brought down here.

THE CELLARS

The extensive cellars under the mansion are full of spiderwebs, barrels, wine bottles and other junk.

One of the cellars is lined with the same Dimensional Shunt circuits as the characters saw earlier. This is how Sir Arnold reaches the pocket dimension. Throwing a big switch on the wall shunts the characters into the pocket dimension.

Also lurking in the cellar on occasion is Zoroth, in the body of one of Sir Arnold's former servants. Zoroth shuffles away from the characters rather than confront them. The characters may glimpse a withered creature with faintly luminescent skin shambling away from them, but when they try pursuing him, he stumbles away into the Shunt room and vanishes. If the characters pursue him through the Shunt, move onto **Scene 7: The Ghost Engine**.

MEETING SIR ARNOLD

Sir Arnold Heath, industrialist and genius engineer, comes across as a little bit nervous and guilty. He's completely ill-at-ease in his fine suit, although he tries to come across as sophisticated and distinguished.

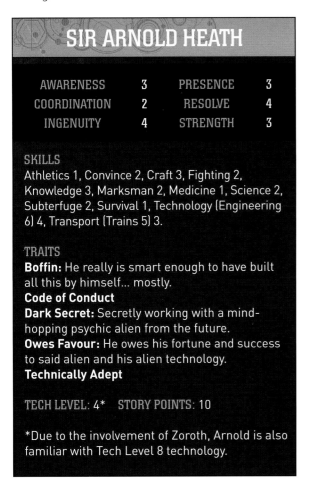

SIR ARNOLD HEATH

AWARENESS	3	PRESENCE	3
COORDINATION	2	RESOLVE	4
INGENUITY	4	STRENGTH	3

SKILLS
Athletics 1, Convince 2, Craft 3, Fighting 2, Knowledge 3, Marksman 2, Medicine 1, Science 2, Subterfuge 2, Survival 1, Technology (Engineering 6) 4, Transport (Trains 5) 3.

TRAITS
Boffin: He really is smart enough to have built all this by himself... mostly.
Code of Conduct
Dark Secret: Secretly working with a mind-hopping psychic alien from the future.
Owes Favour: He owes his fortune and success to said alien and his alien technology.
Technically Adept

TECH LEVEL: 4*   STORY POINTS: 10

*Due to the involvement of Zoroth, Arnold is also familiar with Tech Level 8 technology.

Playing Arnold
- You feel monstrously blessed – you've got a career and wealth beyond your wildest dreams, and you got them by making a horrible, unforgivable mistake. The only way you can live with yourself is by tracking down the Monster.
- You're a 19th century geek, interested in the latest scientific developments. Your partner, Zoroth, has hinted of the great sweep of future history and the wonders of the cosmos. You dream of the great ages to come.
- Even after all these years, you don't know what to make of Zoroth. He's the foundation of all

your success, and he's a being millions of times smarter and wiser than you are – but he's a little... unsettling.
- Be nervous in your body language, and try to overcompensate for everything. Make choppy hand gestures, tap nervously on the table, squirm in your seat.

SIR ARNOLD'S TALE

Sir Arnold's no fool – as soon as the characters mention strange events in the tunnels, or the unusual design of his trains, or alien spaceships, then he realises that he is dealing with uncommon people. He tells the characters that his partner warned him that he would be visited by knowledgeable strangers. Zoroth is expecting the characters – but first, Sir Arnold must explain what's going on.

Heath tells the characters the following:

- Some years ago, he was working as an engineer. They were digging a tunnel near Marnock, and the diggers came to an obstacle they couldn't break through.
- Heath decided to use a small charge of dynamite to smash through. He was careless and didn't properly check his figures. The explosion brought down the tunnel. A dozen miners died.
- Heath was trapped in the collapsed tunnel with another engineer, Solomon Hollis. The blast cleared the earth away from the "obstacle"; it was a strange vessel from another world! The explosion damaged the containment systems on the ship and let the prisoners on board escape.
- The ship, you see, was a prison ship, like the transport that brought prisoners to Australia in Sir Arnold's father's time.
- Some of the prisoners were the Kith, the bat-like things encountered earlier by the characters.
- Another prisoner, though, was something far, far worse. A monster, an abomination, a veritable devil! A demon from hell or a thing from the furtherest reaches of the cosmos, call it what you will, it must be stopped! (Get really emotional at this point. Show the guilt).
- Fortunately, help was at hand. The gaoler was also on board. He – it – was a non-corporeal entity, a Conciliator named Zoroth. Zoroth was gravely wounded in the crash, so he was forced to take the body of Solomon Hollis.
- The prisoner, Peqod, is still at large, but they are close on its trail. Zoroth trapped it with a clever stratagem. Through advanced science, he turned the railways of England into an inescapable net. The prisoner cannot escape this net, and

it draws ever tighter – but Zoroth is growing weak, and may need the help of travellers such as the characters. Sir Arnold will introduce the characters to his strange friend, if they will do him the honour of accompanying him to the Ghost Engine.

If questioned, Arnold admits:

- Zoroth must possess humans to communicate. These hosts rarely last more than a year or two – his power burns them up from within.

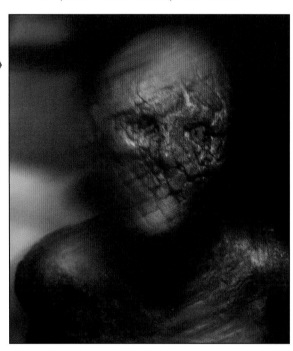

- Zoroth has assembled an army to hunt down the prisoner. Most of his servants are former train workers or soldiers, given new strength by Zoroth's science. When one of the company spies spots the Kith or Peqod, the Hunting Train is dispatched to the scene with all haste.
- Arnold genuinely has no idea about how the characters could have been shunted from the future, or what might have happened to Simon. He suggests they ask Zoroth.

Arnold then leads the characters downstairs to the cellar, and shunts them all into the pocket dimension.

OPTIONAL ENCOUNTER: JENNY'S UNCLE PAUL

Jenny's Uncle Paul went away to sea in his youth, and lost touch with his family. A falling mast took his arm in the South Seas, and he returned to England on his tiny pension. The characters can either encounter

him as one of the Steamborgs guarding the mansion, or as a guest at the benefit dinner at Railway House. Paul recognises Jenny – she's got her mother's eyes and mouth – and greets her. She's the first member of the family he's seen in years.

Paul's either a drunken, sentimental old sot, or a devoted supporter of the Encompassing Company for restoring his missing arm with a brass-and-wire prosthesis. Paul can either be used as a way to get the characters out of a jam, or to make the Encompassing Railway Company more sympathetic, or just to kill time if you need to slow things down.

⚙ 6. THE STOLEN PASSENGERS

The dinner at Railway House is for unfortunates and orphans, and the characters don't qualify under normal circumstances. If they want, they can lurk in disguise with Subterfuge or bluff their way in. Alternatively, they can pose as charitable donors, here to support the cause. Several ladies of good background patronise the cause, in the hopes of catching the eye of Sir Arnold.

Bert the Watchman is on the guest list, as are many other workmen and soldiers, especially those who have lost limbs or suffered other grievous wounds. Before the dinner, officials from the Encompassing Company circulate through the crowd, asking questions of the guests. How did you suffer your injury? What was your profession before you were so afflicted? Some of the questions, though, are rather odd, like "how often do you dream?" or "can you guess what's on this card?" – they're testing for low-level psychic ability! Zoroth prefers hosts that won't fight back.

As part of the dinner, the Company has arranged special trains and Hackney cabs to bring people home. Those who *fail* the test are given yellow tickets for the return train. Those who pass are given red tickets.

The dinner itself is unremarkable; the food is cheap but hearty, and the speech by Mrs Faberlin on the spiritual virtues of physical toil is so full of obscure classical allusions that the diners can happily ignore it instead of pretending to listen.

OPTIONAL ENCOUNTER: INSPECTOR CRANNELL

The Inspector can show up here again if Madame Vastra is here; he suspects she's stalking new victims. Could she be a vampire, with Jenny as

her sapphic thrall? Who, then, is this stranger who behaves so oddly and claims to be more than a thousand years old? Could he be the master vampire? (Inspector Crannell may have read too much Gothic fiction).

By the way, if you run with the vampire gag, then remember the Kith are bat-winged monsters...

AFTER THE DINNER

The injured people who got yellow tickets are herded to a special underground train by the Encompassing Railway staff. This train rattles off into a tunnel... and vanishes in a flare of blue light. If the characters are on board, then they're transported into the Ghost Engine. If they're not on board, then they can chase after the train – the Dimensional Shunt circuits are still 'hot' so the characters can easily follow it through, just like they got dragged through the shunt at Marnock.

Alternatively, the characters can go off to Heath's mansion to ask questions there (see **Scene 5: Heath's Mansion**).

⚙ 7. THE GHOST ENGINE

The characters find themselves inside the Ghost Engine.

It's something out of the fever dream of an engineer. Imagine a cavern or a sea made of blue fire. In this cavern is a titanic engine, cobbled together from

locomotive parts and scrap iron. This engine is so huge that people live in a shanty town of lean-tos and huts in and around its monstrously big boilers and gearshafts. At the heart of the engine, connected to it by thick cables, is an alien starship like a silver-green jewel. Dozens of the Steamborg engineers toil to maintain this great groaning engine.

At the foot of the engine is a train station where a single strange train waits. It's the Hunting Train that the characters might have glimpsed in the underground tunnels.

WELCOMING COMMITTEE

If the characters arrive here in the company of Sir Arnold, then he shows them around briefly before bringing them to Zoroth.

If they snuck in here, then they need to hide before the Steamborgs take them prisoner. A Coordination + Subterfuge test (Difficulty 18) lets them hide long enough to spy on the machinery before Zoroth senses them and sends Sir Arnold plus a detachment of armed Steamborgs to detain them.

If Sir Arnold hasn't already monologued at the characters (see **Sir Arnold's Tale**, above), then he does so now.

THE MACHINERY

There are four distinct devices here, identifiable by anyone with a high Science skill (characters familiar with advanced technology, such as the Doctor or Madame Vastra, don't need to roll; other characters can roll Ingenuity + Science to make a guess).

- First, there's the starship. It's right in the middle of this pocket dimension, so it's a reasonable guess that it's somehow generating this little reality bubble. The Doctor can identify it on sight as a Conciliator Prison Capsule – the Conciliator would possess the living ship and pilot its prisoners back to the wastelands of time and leave them there.
  - The ship's damaged. Probably from an explosion right against a vulnerable section.
- Second, there's the machinery surrounding the starship. Parts of it rotate slowly around the Conciliator ship; other sections clearly provide power for it. It's the source of the Hyperyon particles that open the Dimensional Shunts; it's also somehow wired into the rails themselves. It's connected right to the railway network of England.
- Third, there's the Hunting Train. It looks like a military train, with armoured flanks and gunports.
  - A close examination of the train shows that it's got some sort of electromagnetic gizmo built into it, like a cage. It's obviously designed to contain something. (It's for trapping Peqod.)
- Finally, there's the foundry where Zoroth converts people into Steamborgs. As creating cyborgs with 19th century technology is virtually impossible, Zoroth performs the surgery personally, using his far-future skills to accomplish the virtually impossible time and time again.

ZOROTH

Zoroth's in the foundry directly beneath the ship. He's currently possessing the body of a middle-aged man; his skin is deathly pale, almost translucent, and his eyes glow an eerie green. He moves like an ancient, brittle man.

- If the characters are sneaking around, then he senses them and addresses them by name. (Optionally, run **A Sighting** first). Make him seem distant and inhuman, but not wholly unpleasant – he's posing as a higher intelligence from the far future (when he's actually a crazy, space-conquering higher intelligence from the far future).
- If they're introduced to him by Sir Arnold, then he greets them in his alien way, and claims to have been expecting them.

Playing Zoroth:

- Try to come across as an angel; a scary biblical angel, the ones who say "be not afraid" because they're terrifying and awful and turn into wheels of fire. You're nearly as powerful as a Time Lord, and a lot more arrogant!
- You're trapped on this ghastly planet. You desperately want to get back to the future and start sowing chaos again – but your only way out is to recapture Peqod, and your only way to do that is to pretend to be a Conciliator, and pretend you're a boring member of the Constant, and that you care for these stupid apes.
- Justify any of your more questionable decisions by saying its for the greater good.
- Zoroth's plan is to capture Peqod, torture him until he gives up the codes to control the starship, then return to the far future and start his rebellion again. If Zoroth learns that the characters have a time machine, he may try to capture the TARDIS or steal their Vortex Manipulator instead – any way to the future works for him!
- Sometimes, if you're pressed, let the mask slip. Let your anger – your terrible anger, fierce enough to sear planets like a supernova – show through.
- Hold your body completely still, as though it might crack.

Talking to Zoroth: The alien dispassionately tells the characters what's going on – or a very edited version, anyway.

- He tells them he is a Conciliator from the Constant of Harmony (if he's speaking to a character unfamiliar with the far future, then he may have to explain all that too).
- He piloted a prison ship into the past, but something went wrong and they crashed here on Earth.
- The Kith creatures were on the ship, but the really dangerous prisoner was a creature called Peqod – a renegade Conciliator. In the far future, this Peqod launched a terrible destructive war that nearly brought down the Constant of Harmony. The Conciliators captured Peqod and banished him. Now he's escaped, and must be recaptured.
- Peqod could use his time travel ability to return to the far future, but Zoroth was able to cobble together a way to stop him – he turned the railways of England into a huge antennae that confined Peqod. He's out there somewhere within the area bounded by the Encompassing Railway.

GHOST ENGINES

- Zoroth needs the characters' help. So far, Peqod has managed to elude him. His spies and Steamborgs keep looking for Peqod, but every time they spot him, Peqod escapes.
- Zoroth expected time travellers to show up at some point; he's meddled in the normal progression of the 19th century. He'll try to learn all he can, then steal their time machine if it's an option.

IT DOESN'T ADD UP

Observant or paranoid players may spot some inconsistencies in Zoroth's claims. They're quite right...

- **Why not return to the future and get more Conciliators to help?** Zoroth says that Peqod somehow damaged his power to time travel.
- **Why use the Encompassing Railway? Why the Steamborgs?** The primitives are disposable tools. Recapturing Peqod is more important than any individual human life. Zoroth regrets the necessity.
- **Why possess hosts?** The only way to recapture Peqod is to work through physical means. It needs these hosts.
- **What about the hosts he's using?** Again, humans are disposable. Peqod is a monster that can stride from world to world and time to time, like a glorious god in comparison to these apes. The hosts' lives are sacrifices for the greater good.

A SIGHTING

One of the Steamborgs hurries up to Zoroth. There's been a sighting! They saw the Monster in the tunnels near Marnock, near the crash site. It wasn't like before – previously, the Monster was like a shimmering ghost, but this time it was possessing the body of a child.

From the description, it's clearly possessing Simon!

Zoroth claims that his technology can free the child from possession. The characters must capture Simon/Peqod and restrain him in the electromagnetic cage in the Hunting Train, then bring him back here where Zoroth will... extract the prisoner using the Ghost Engine. It will not be pleasant for the child, but he may survive.

THE GAME'S AFOOT

Zoroth urges the characters to board the Hunting Train along with his Steamborgs. The Steamborgs

are loyal servants, but he fears that they will be unable to catch Peqod. The characters may have better luck.

If some of the characters choose to stay behind, then Zoroth may try to force or trick them into revealing the location of their time machine.

Sir Arnold accompanies the characters on their hunt. He rarely accompanies the hunts these days, but this is the best sighting they've had in years. Finally, finally, their target may be within sight.

What Can the Monster Do? The characters may wish to know what they're up against. Zoroth tells them that the child has the powers of a full Conciliator; inhuman strength, speed and toughness, powerful telepathic abilities, force shields and power to blast you with psychic energy. Their only hope, claims Zoroth, is to wear the protective suits (so the monster cannot warp their minds or possess their bodies) and blast the child with gunshots until its shields are exhausted, then capture it in the Ghost Cage.

- Ask the players if they're going to put on the protective suits offered by Zoroth.

GHOST ENGINES

TROUBLESHOOTING: HEY, HE'S A BAD GUY

It's possible that the players realise that Zoroth's a villain earlier in the game. If so, then the final scenes switch from "help Zoroth recapture Peqod" to "get to Peqod before Zoroth". Push the characters into stealing one of the trains and zooming off with it.

⚙ 8. THE HUNTING EXPEDITION

The Hunting Train rattles through the night. It emerges from a Dimensional Shunt in the same tunnel where the characters first entered the 19th century, and roars on into the countryside (seeding the legends of the ghost train that drew Simon to the tunnel in the first places). According to the sighting, one of the Encompassing Railway signalmen at Marnock saw the Monster running down the railway track, and Zoroth told them that it cannot stray far from the rails.

OPTIONAL ENCOUNTER: MORE KITH

The characters spot the distinctive flapping silhouettes of the Kith up ahead. The Kith circle around the train before one of the monsters lands on the roof. It squeals that it wants to talk:

"Meat will listen. Meat will speak to the Kith. This is a pleasant time for us. Lots to eat. Lots to hunt. You will not take us away. We make bargain. Bargain. Show you where Peqod is, and you promise to let us stay here and hunt forever."

The Kith claims to be able to find Peqod. In exchange for this secret, they want a solemn promise that the characters will let them stay here in London, feasting on humans.

If the characters accept, the Kith cackle. "Meat is wise. Meat is clever. Follow." The Kith tell the characters to take a side track, claiming that they saw Peqod down this rail line. "Faster", they urge, "faster. He's getting away."

- The Kith are trying to trick the characters – this siding crosses a railway viaduct that the Kith have sabotaged. They intend to destroy the train.
- Call for Awareness + Craft rolls (Difficulty 15) to notice that this railway siding is unfinished, or Awareness + Ingenuity to spot the half-eaten bodies of railway workers hidden in the trees that flash past the racing train.
- If all the checks fail, then the characters don't have time to stop the train safely when it comes around the bend and they see the crumbling viaduct.

- Once the characters work out that they're heading for disaster, they can try to stop the train by slamming on the brakes. The Kith will try to stop them. If the train does go over the edge, then the characters can jump clear at the last moment. The containment system survives the crash, but will have to be hastily repaired.

If they refuse, then the Kith attack the train, trying to wriggle in through the gunports and tear through the hatches. The Kith are desperate; they fear that the characters will make contact with Peqod and learn the truth.

- This is horror-movie territory: giant space vampire bats on a train. The Kith are strong enough to tear metal.
- Throw a Story Point at the first player to make a comment along the lines of "I have had it with these bats on this train."
- Remember to include Sir Arnold and the Steamborgs in the fight – don't bother rolling dice for them, but describe their actions.
- If the characters get into trouble, bring in Peqod.

CATCHING THE MONSTER

The characters spot a strange glowing figure standing on the rail tracks ahead. It's Simon. He's obviously possessed by something: he's surrounded by an aura of light. He looks exhausted, though, the same drawn expression and pale skin that the characters saw earlier in Zoroth's host. He's waiting for them.

Here's how things go down if the characters **don't** intervene:

- Sir Arnold orders the Steamborgs to open fire. There's a barrage of gunfire. Most of it bounces off Simon/Peqod's protective aura, but it staggers the child.
- Simon tries fighting back, sending tendrils of psychic energy at the train, but the Steamborgs' protective suits make them immune to him.
- Another barrage of fire knocks him over. Other Steamborgs swarm out of the train, pick him up, and imprison him in the cage.

The character may try other tactics, like tricking Peqod into surrendering.

More likely, the characters will try talking to Simon/Peqod, or protecting him. The aura fades as Peqod lets Simon take control of their shared body. Simon's obviously terrified, but says "the policeman" helped him. He asks the characters to listen to the policeman.

Sir Arnold & The Monster: Remember that Sir Arnold's obsessed with capturing Peqod. If the characters stop him, he has a breakdown, the stiff upper lip crumbling completely. "You don't understand! It has to be stopped! I've got to do it for them! That's why I'm still alive! That's why I'm alive!" The players can talk him down through good roleplaying or good Presence + Convince rolls.

- This is a chance for the characters to put Sir Arnold back on the path of redemption.

Playing Peqod: Peqod assumes control of Simon's body to talk to the players. The Conciliator recognises the Doctor, if present, and will address any Time Lord with deference.

- Play Peqod as a stern, inhuman force; a warrior angel, perhaps.
- "I am Conciliator Peqod. I was forced to take this host. The child is under my protection."
- Explaing that you're a Conciliator. You travelled into the past with exiled prisoners, but there was an accident and your ship crashed. The prisoners escaped.
- You were piloting the ship through the Time Vortex when it crashed. You were entangled with the ship's psychic circuits, and it took you some time to disentangle yourself. You tried to return to the future, but found yourself dragged back here. Somehow, Zoroth has managed to create a time trap.
- Zoroth's a monster; a renegade Conciliator, the leader of a revolutionary army. He's brainwashed billions into serving him. He can implant psychic controls in lesser beings, turning them into extensions of his will. He must be stopped.
- You tried to resist taking a host, but you were injured in the crash. You had no choice. He may be dying. You cannot leave Simon's body without external assistance.
  - Peqod *could*, maybe, with a Psychic character's help, jump into another character's body instead.
  - Alternatively, one of the characters could give up part of their life force to help the Conciliator.
  - Or they could suggest that Sir Arnold atone that way.

Zoroth's Revenge: As soon as it becomes clear that the characters aren't going to capture Peqod and deliver him in a nice cage, or as soon as the

characters realise that Zoroth was the prisoner, not Peqod, then Zoroth goes to his backup plan. All of the Steamborgs suddenly freeze in place and start talking in unison.

"Damn you! Couldn't you apes have done one thing right? All I wanted to do was make the Constant burn... and I still shall! You will bring me the Conciliator... or I'll make this primitive planet into a graveyard! You think these primitives can beat me?"

Zoroth can remotely control the Steamborgs. They start closing on the characters and Peqod...

⚙ 9. TERMINUS

End of the line. How do the characters get out of this one?

There are several problems facing the characters. The immediate one is the squad of Steamborgs closing in around them, but that's just a combat scene – resourceful characters can easily deal with that!

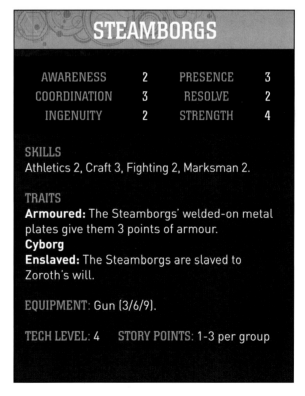

STEAMBORGS

AWARENESS	2	PRESENCE	3
COORDINATION	3	RESOLVE	2
INGENUITY	2	STRENGTH	4

SKILLS
Athletics 2, Craft 3, Fighting 2, Marksman 2.

TRAITS
Armoured: The Steamborgs' welded-on metal plates give them 3 points of armour.
Cyborg
Enslaved: The Steamborgs are slaved to Zoroth's will.

EQUIPMENT: Gun (3/6/9).

TECH LEVEL: 4   **STORY POINTS:** 1-3 per group

Next, they've got to decide how to stop Zoroth. There are several potential ways to do that:

- Stop Zoroth's army of Steamborgs by collapsing the dimensional pocket.
- Use the hunting train to capture Zoroth.

GHOST ENGINES

- Tricking Zoroth somehow – say, by claiming to have the control codes for the ship, then locking him in there.
- Get Peqod back to the far future to call in help from the Conciliators:
  - Either by getting back to the TARDIS and travelling there.
  - Or by heading back to the Ghost Engine and sabotaging the time trap that prevents Peqod from returning to the far future.

All these plans likely involve stealing the Hunting Train and heading back into the pocket dimension. Zoroth controls the Dimensional Shunts, but the characters can either use Jiggery-Pokery to open them, or Sir Arnold can suggest reaching the Ghost Engine via the secret portal in the cellars of his mansion.

Whatever plan the characters come up with probably has a fair chance of working. Here are some factors that might play into it:

Zoroth's Steamborgs: Zoroth's got an arbitrarily large army of Steamborgs, and he'll keep making more by kidnapping underground trains via Dimensional Shunts. He's not able to maintain direct control over all of them – he's much weaker than he is in the future, but he can still control a dozen or so at once. Once he's got enough, he intends to march them out via the Dimensional Shunts and start conquering London. He doesn't particularly want to conquer London or kill all the humans. He's just being petty about this.

Many of the Steamborgs wear protective suits to block Peqod's telepathy. A Boffin might be able to adjust the frequency of the suits, so they block Zoroth instead.

The Ghost Engine: The Ghost Engine runs the dimensional pocket, the shunts and keeps Peqod from time travelling. It's powered by electricity cables from Sir Arnold's mansion (although there's a back-up steam generator) and is connected to the crashed Conciliator ship (which has the dimension manipulation/time travel elements). The characters can stop it by blowing it up (which takes a lot of force, like crashing a train into it) or by running around inside it pulling the right levers.

Destroying the Ghost Engine may cause the dimensional pocket to collapse.

The Conciliator Ship: Zoroth's repaired the damage to it, but needs the control codes to fly it.

The Conciliators: If the characters make contact with the Conciliators, then the scary space ghost police zoom back in time and possess all of the human characters. Take their players aside for a moment and explain that they're playing scary space ghosts who are going to deus ex machina in and zap Zoroth.

CONCILIATORS, ZOROTH AND PEQOD

AWARENESS	4	PRESENCE	7
COORDINATION	3	RESOLVE	6
INGENUITY	6	STRENGTH	4

SKILLS
Athletics 3, Craft 4, Fighting 2, Marksman 3, Science 6, Technology 5.

TRAITS
Alien
Impervious: Conciliators can use their mental powers to generate a psychic forcefield of sorts, shifting any physical damage results down by one step.
Psychic
Possess: To manifest physically the Conciliators must possess a human being. Zoroth's crime was using this power to mind control multiple creatures at once.
Telekinesis
Telepathy
Vortex: When not trapped in the past by spectral railways or pseudo-imprisonment, the Conciliators can travel freely through time.

TECH LEVEL: 8   STORY POINTS: 8

✹ AFTERMATH

Once Zoroth's defeated, it's time to wrap up. Questions that you and your players might still have to answer:

- Is Simon returned to the future?
- What happened to the other missing people? Did they get turned into Steamborgs or burnt up as hosts for Zoroth and Peqod?
- What happens to Sir Arnold and the Steamborgs? Can they be rehabilitated, perhaps together?
- What's the fate of Zoroth? Is it really a good idea to banish him into the past? Might he one day escape to trouble the characters once more…?

THE NORTHERN KNIGHTS

This story takes a group of characters back in time, to England in the reign of Queen Elizabeth I. There a sinister alliance threatens the soul of both England and Scotland.

A Cybermen Scout Ship crashed in Hawksfordshire and the Cybermen have formed a secret alliance with the rebellious Earl of Hawksford. The characters arrive in Mortenbury, where the Cybermats are spreading a plague to isolate Baron Mortenbury and his guest, Mary, Queen of Scots. What interest has the Earl in Mary and what are the Cybermen really up to in Hawkwood?

✸ ADVENTURE SYNOPSIS

For whatever reason, the characters decide to take a jaunt back to Tudor England. Perhaps the Doctor is taking Clara back to the 5th century to prove that there was no real King Arthur, missing the date by a thousand years.

Maybe they fancy teaming up with Robin Hood and his Merry Men for a jovial jaunt once again. Perhaps the Doctor's decided to try to make amends with his former wife, Queen Elizabeth I. Or, maybe this is just one of those times when the TARDIS takes them where they need to go, not necessarily where they want to go.

Whatever the reason, the TARDIS arrives in the north of England, in 1575. There they encounter a physician, Dr Gabriel Field, who is tending to the victims of a mysterious plague. The characters take shelter in the castle of Lord Percival, where they meet Mary, Queen of Scots, held prisoner there on the orders of Queen Elizabeth I. Finding his garrison depleted by the plague too, they uncover the source – it is being spread by Cybermats! – and find his enemy, Lord Tristan, planning to lay siege to the castle. Resisting the siege, they uncover that the Cybermen have allied themselves with Lord Tristan, and are turning the victims of the plague into new Cybermen from their crashed spaceship.

✸ THE CYBERMEN'S PLAN

En route to Earth in the 21st century, a Cyber Scout Ship was caught in a Temporal Wake of the Time War and cast back in time, crashing in Hawksfordshire, Northern England, in 1575. Unfortunately for them, their vessel was drained of power and they were forced to make a crash landing. The ion drive was damaged but not completely destroyed; while the spaceship is permanently grounded, the two Cybermen piloting the vessel could still draw power from it.

The Cybermen immediately activated an emergency beacon and sent a mobile solar converter into geosynchronous orbit to fuel the ion drive. They also released Cybermats to scout the area. The crawling metal scouts spotted Lord Tristan and his guard approaching the spaceship. The Cybermen negotiated with Lord Tristan and received his protection and resources in return for their help taking control of England. Lord Tristan was partially converted into a Cyberman as well.

Drunk with his new strength and potential power – not to mention somewhat unhinged from the partial conversion – Lord Tristan believes that the Cybermen are 'warrior angels' come to help him claim England for the Holy See by taking Mary Stuart as his bride. In truth, the Cybermen patiently await reinforcements from their Cyber-fleet as they make long-term plans to turn Earth into a Cybermen factory. Fortunately, they need to replicate several generations' worth of scientific advances before they can initiate large-scale conversion.

The Cybermen have been extremely active in the week since they've arrived. They have enacted a plan to isolate Mary in Mortenbury for Lord Tristan's benefit. Cybermats have been spreading a plague, isolating Mortenbury castle. Those who succumb to their plague become vulnerable to a form of mind control using elevated iron and sulphur levels in their bloodstream and powerful magnetic fields, before eventually falling victim to full Cyber-conversion. Lord Tristan has also been active, secretly spreading word to recusant allies to be prepared to fight for Mary.

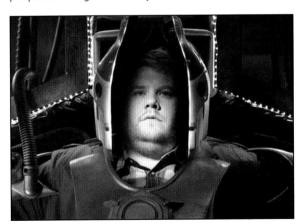

The falling star, a strange new plague and Lord Tristan's boasting amongst his Catholic allies has not gone unnoticed. Francis Walsingham, Secretary to Elizabeth, has sent an agent to ascertain the truth of a rumoured plot to free Mary and, if true, to bring the evidence to him. Unfortunately his agent, Dr Gabriel Field, is a bit overzealous and plans to assassinate Mary if her escape seems imminent.

✸ RELIGION AND THE NORTH

Religion is a divisive issue during Elizabeth's reign. For the last quarter of a century England had swapped back and forth between Roman Catholicism and the Church of England as its state religion (the Anglican Church itself was being pulled in different directions too, as some wished it to adhere to Roman Catholic traditions while others wanted it to become more radically Protestant). This came to a head during Roman Catholic Mary I's reign, where 'Bloody Mary' had 284 'heretics' executed.

During Anglican Elizabeth's reign many of her subjects continue to practice Roman Catholicism, especially in Northern England. These subjects are known as 'recusants' and usually pay a fee to be exempt from Anglican services. Some recusants don't see Elizabeth as a legitimate queen and get embroiled in plots, sometimes with France and Spain, to replace her with a Catholic monarch. One of the potential replacements is Mary Stuart – Mary, Queen of Scots – who fled Scotland in the face of Protestant discontent. Elizabeth has had her imprisoned, but doesn't know what to do with her. In the meantime Elizabeth's Privy Council sees the recusants as a threat and Mary as a potential rallying point. Both the Northern Rebellion of 1569 and the exposed Ridolfi Plot the following year tried to replace Elizabeth with Mary. Today, Principal Secretary Francis Walsingham is using secret agents to expose similar threats and, hopefully, connect enough evidence that Mary was behind these plots to persuade Elizabeth to execute her.

SEPARATING FACT FROM FICTION

Like many of the Doctor's historical jaunts, **The Northern Knights** is a historical adventure with fictional elements. Mary Stuart really is in the custody of the Earl of Shrewsbury and the Earl did move her between his various castles and manors. However, Mortenbury and Hawksfordshire are fictional places and Baron Mortenbury and the Earl of Hawksfordshire are fictional people. The creation of fictional elements gives the Gamemaster a free hand in blowing up castles and raising a body count without worrying about changing history. If anything happens to Mary Stuart, of course, history is changed, but that is as it should be. The players need something that raises the stakes when confronting the Cybermen.

⚙ 1. AN EPIDEMIC OF UNEARTHLY PROPORTIONS

The TARDIS drops the characters into an English riverside village where they meet Dr Gabriel Field. Gabriel tells them of the strange plague occurring in this region and the group may learn that the plague is alien in origin. Gabriel asks them to accompany him to Mortenbury Castle for the night.

THE DOCTORS MEET

The TARDIS has landed in a stable in Mortenbury, a village in Shropshire. Its arrival has spooked the horses and they flee the barn as the TARDIS materialises. This has garnered the attention of Dr Gabriel Field, a physician that is ministering to the plague-ridden villagers. Gabriel heard "a most sinister sound" coming from the stable and, with the horses bolting, wonders if there is black magic afoot.

Read or paraphrase the following, adjusting as necessary for your group:

The moment you exit the TARDIS you smell the intense stench of manure. It appears that the ship has materialised inside a stable, judging by the amount of hay strewn about. The animals appear to have bolted, as the stable doors hang loosely from their hinges.

As the characters look around, have them make an Awareness + Ingenuity roll (Difficulty 15). Read the following to those that make it:

As you look at the hanging doors, leathery fingers grip one of them and slowly pull it open. A leathery head with a long beak and large, glassy eyes peers round from behind the door.

This 'creature' is Dr Gabriel Field, an English physician who is wearing typical field gear for entering a plague-ridden village: he is wearing a long cloak with a robe beneath, a hood and hat covering his head and a mask covering his face. The inside of the beak is filled with oils that are supposed to ward off plague.

In addition to gloves he also wears a number of charms, some of which have magical significance. His cloak is soaked in vinegar, which a character with a Keen Sense of smell immediately picks up. He also carries a rapier for protection, although he does not threaten the group with it.

Once Gabriel realises that he's been spotted he makes no aggressive moves. Indeed, he is just as curious about the group as they are of him, especially if they are not wearing period clothing. He will attempt to convince them that he means no harm by holding out his hands. Assuming that the group takes no aggressive action, he speaks with a muffled voice.

"Have you the plague?"

If any of the characters have the Alien Appearance trait, they will look 'odd' enough to be considered plague victims. The players will need to come up

with an appropriate story (and skill roll) to convince Gabriel that they are clean.

As the characters can tell by the bobbing of his beak he is taking their measure, looking them up and down and then from side to side. His mask stops as he sees the strange blue box that is woefully out of place in a stable.

"Are you agents of the Principal Secretary? I hear his eyes and ears are in Shropshire these days."

The Principal Secretary is Francis Walsingham, who has spies in Shropshire rooting out foreign agents and their supporters. Gabriel does not reveal that he is working for Walsingham himself.

Once the characters have verified that they do not have the plague and are not agents of Walsingham, Gabriel nods and removes his mask, revealing a young man in his late twenties with his blonde hair cropped short.

WHY, YES WE DO WORK FOR WALSINGHAM

The characters might make a bold gamble and admit that they are agents of Walsingham – if they use their Psychic Paper, it'll show such credentials to Gabriel whether they want to or not. In this case, Gabriel sees them as allies and admits that he is an agent as well, although he still won't admit to his plan to murder Mary Stuart. He hopes to use them surreptitiously to aid his scheme.

"A pleasure to meet you, then, even in a place like this. I am Dr Gabriel Field of Shrewsbury. Forgive me if I don't shake your hand but I shouldn't find that prudent."

If asked, Gabriel verifies that they are in England in the spring of 1575. He has come up from Shrewsbury

to investigate a strange plague that is afflicting the region. Gabriel knows that Mary Stuart is in Mortenbury Castle but won't mention it. He is keen to get information from the group as their manner and style suggests that they may be foreign agents.

He'll ask them their business in Mortenbury, a village that has been particularly hard hit by the plague. Gabriel is concerned because Mortenbury is generally closed except to physicians, of which few are entering the village.

DR GABRIEL FIELD

AWARENESS	4	PRESENCE	4
COORDINATION	3	RESOLVE	3
INGENUITY	4	STRENGTH	2

Gabriel Field is a Shrewsbury physician who is secretly working for Francis Walsingham. If approached about this he will only break his cover if he trusts the characters. Otherwise, he just offers heated denials and misdirection. While not explicitly ordered to do so by Walsingham (he merely impressed upon Gabriel the dire necessity to keep Mary out of Northern hands), Dr Field plans on killing Mary rather than allow her to escape.

SKILLS
Athletics 2, Convince 3, Craft 4, Fighting 2, Knowledge 4, Marksman 3, Medicine 5, Science 4, Subterfuge 3, Survival 2, Technology 2, Transport 2.

TRAITS
Brave: Gabriel walks among plague victims regularly, risking his own health. He gets a +2 bonus to any resolve roll in which he needs to show courage.
Dark Secret: Gabriel is a secret agent working for Principal Secretary Francis Walsingham. This secret can get him killed if revealed to the recusants (see pg. 27).
Empathic: Gabriel is good at reading people. He gets +2 bonus on rolls to empathise with or read another person.

EQUIPMENT: Wagon, two field dresses, other clothes, medicines, magic charms, rapier (Strength +2 in combat).

TECH LEVEL: 3   **STORY POINTS:** 6

THE NORTHERN KNIGHTS

A MOST ALIEN PLAGUE

Inquisitive characters may want to see the symptoms of this plague (don't worry if they don't, there'll be more victims to examine later). Gabriel warns them that they should be fully attired if they wish to examine a victim and offers them his spare field dress. Gabriel has just come from the village blacksmith Ronald, whose apprentice Geoffrey has contracted the plague, so that seems a good place to start.

Gabriel knocks on the door and an older man opens it. The two exchange pleasantries and after Gabriel explains the situation Ronald lets them in. Like everyone else whose contracted this plague, Geoffrey caught it while he slept.

Geoffrey lies in bed; he looks feverish and Ronald says he only stirs on occasion and babbles incoherently. His hand is bandaged; Gabriel mentions that he cut Geoffrey's hand to determine whether he had the current plague. The cut confirmed it.

If a character asks why then Gabriel carefully unwraps Geoffrey's hand and shows the group the blood stain on the bandage: it's dark green.

At this point, characters who make an Awareness + Medicine roll (Difficulty 15) and are familiar with Tech Level 5 or above recognise the blood discolouration as sulfemoglobinemia, or too much sulphur in the blood. While it can be caused by overdosing on certain medications in the late 20th century, it shouldn't be present in 1575. What plague puts sulphur in the blood?

Suspicious characters who look around may, with an Awareness + Subterfuge or Survival roll (Difficulty 18), notice a trail across the dirt floor like something came from an open window to Geoffrey's bed (this is a Cybermat trail). A character giving Geoffrey a thorough examination finds, with an Awareness and Medicine roll (Difficulty 12), a break in Geoffrey's skin on his shoulder. He was either bitten by or injected with something.

If the characters have Gabriel take them to other victims in Mortenbury they discover similar clues. Obviously, someone is infecting the villagers deliberately. An Awareness and Survival roll (Difficulty 15) outside reveals the tracks as well.

Mortenbury's church, St Mathias', is being run by Cerdic Chandler, the churchwarden. Cerdic has been holding the church together this past week after Vicar Godfrey Simpson fell ill. So far he has had to perform a couple of funerals himself with the Vicar's fevered blessing. When speaking to the characters Cerdic is a nervous wreck and asks to be left alone.

CERDIC CHANDLER

AWARENESS	3	PRESENCE	4
COORDINATION	4	RESOLVE	3
INGENUITY	3	STRENGTH	2

Now in his forties, Cerdic Chandler is a well-respected man in Mortenbury. Not only does he supply the village, the church and castle with candles, but he is also the churchwarden and an alderman. With both Vicar Simpson and Town Mayor Robin Fleet struck down by plague, Cerdic finds himself in control of both the church and the town. He consults frequently with Constable Hugo Bright about keeping the plague contained and getting assistance from other parishes.

Thus far Cerdic has only had to hold three funerals. He knows of the body-snatching rumours but can only confirm that four people have disappeared from their beds at night. He believes this to be the result of vigilante fear and that the bodies have been secretly cremated (very un-Christian like) to burn out the plague.

SKILLS
Athletics 2, Convince 4, Craft 4, Fighting 2, Knowledge 3, Marksman 2, Subterfuge 2, Survival 2, Technology 1, Transport 2..

TRAITS
By the Book: As the enforcer (and in many cases enactor) of laws, Cerdic insists that they be followed. He receives a +2 on Resolve rolls to resist being influenced to break rules, laws, or traditions.
Friends: Normally, Cerdic has many clerical friends throughout the region that he can call upon for aid. Unfortunately, the plague has somewhat diminished this network.
Voice of Authority: Cerdic is well-respected in Mortenbury.

TECH LEVEL: 3   STORY POINTS: 3

THE ALIEN 'PLAGUE'

The plague is not a plague at all, but a poison spread by the Cybermats. It causes feverish conditions and elevates iron and sulphur levels in the bloodstream (giving the Cybermen a bit more control over their victims). The extra iron and sulphur can be diagnosed by a character with an Awareness + Medicine roll (Difficulty 15), assuming familiarity with Technology Level 5.

Fortunately, this poison can be countered effectively and quickly with a stimulant found in coffee. A couple of strong cups of coffee can purge the poison in hours. Unfortunately, coffee is still pretty rare in England at this point.

The poison is generally non-lethal (unless the victim dies from complications with other diseases) and runs its course within a week.

A VISIT TO MORTENBURY CASTLE

At some point, Gabriel suggests that they all find shelter in Mortenbury Castle for the evening. The castle sits on a hill overlooking the town of Mortenbury, which sits along the River Bevern. The castle is owned by Lord Percival Rudwick, the Baron of Mortenbury. He is currently hosting Mary Stuart as a favour to his Lord, the Earl of Shrewsbury, who's been called to London to report her condition to Queen Elizabeth.

Dusk falls over the grey sky as rain pelts the characters' clothes. Two armoured guards holding poleaxes stand silently in the gateway behind the drawbridge. One of them clears his throat and calls out to the characters.

"What business have you with the Baron?"

A character making an Awareness + Ingenuity roll (Difficulty 12) can read the nervousness in the guards' eyes and manner. Something inside has them on edge.

If the characters don't make a pitch then Gabriel does, asking for lodgings for the evening. As a physician, he prides his health, as he would do no patients any good should he contract the disease himself.

"Hah!" says one of the guards. "Then you'd do better to sleep in the woods, for this castle is touched with plague."

In spite of the warning, the guards won't send them away, especially with at least one physician among them. The other guard goes inside to speak with Sir Aldric about allowing the characters to come inside.

MEETING THE CAPTAIN

Sir Aldric arrives as soon as he is informed of the travellers.

The second guard returns with a dashing young man wearing a leather jerkin. He keeps a neat moustache and beard trimmed close while letting his shoulder-length hair hang free. A rapier is tucked into a scabbard by his side and he has one gloved hand resting on the pommel.

"Greetings, travellers!" he says cheerfully. "I am Sir Aldric Hanson, captain of the Castle Guard. As my lord is in dire need of a good physician, he grants you a most warm welcome!"

Sir Aldric offers to personally escort the characters inside. He is especially deferential to any female characters, asking them for the honour of taking them by the hand to personally lead them inside.

As the characters enter the bailey an Awareness + Ingenuity roll (Difficulty 12) makes it readily apparent that the castle is undermanned. Most of the guards that do remain look tired, as if they've been up all night. In truth they have been; most of them were on night duty when the plague ripped through the guard barracks, reducing

the complement from 40 to just 18. Lord Percival has sent messengers to other barons for aid, but he doubts any would risk the plague to come, even with the importance of his current duty (of which Sir Aldric won't explain).

If asked whether the Baron expects an attack, Sir Aldric shrugs and says it's a constant threat, especially with the Hawksfordshire recusants less than a day's ride away. Still, so long as the plague doesn't spread, Sir Aldric feels that the current force, supplemented with able bodies from the town and the fields, can hold the castle against a siege for days, as long as the recusants aren't fielding any cannons.

SIR ALDRIC HANSON

AWARENESS	3	PRESENCE	4
COORDINATION	5	RESOLVE	4
INGENUITY	3	STRENGTH	4

Sir Aldric Hanson comes from a long line of knights and is currently the commander of Baron Mortenbury's guardsmen. Most times he seems more archer than mounted warrior and he considers the use of firearms unseemly (although that has more to do with their inaccuracy than any moral objection). He is a handsome man just past 30 years old.

SKILLS
Athletics 4, Convince 3, Craft 1, Fighting 5, Knowledge 1, Marksman 5, Subterfuge 2, Survival 4, Transport 3.

TRAITS
Attractive: Sir Aldric has roguish good looks and gets +2 bonus on rolls that involve his appearance.
Charming: Sir Aldric has natural charm and gets +2 bonuses to rolls whenever his charm would prove useful.
Quick Reflexes: Sir Aldric has quick reflexes and usually goes first in a fight.

EQUIPMENT: Rapier (+2 Strength in combat), knife, leather jerkin (provides 2 levels of armour protection). In the field he carries a longbow and arrows. He owns a suit of armour (armour 8) but only puts it on for ceremonies.

TECH LEVEL: 3   **STORY POINTS:** 4

AN AUDIENCE WITH THE BARON

After being admitted to the keep, the Baron wishes to learn the characters' true purpose here. Sir Aldric leads the characters into a lavish building, obviously built a bit later than the medieval walls that surround it. He explains to them that this is the residence of Lord Percival Rudwick, the Baron of Mortenbury, who is performing a rather special task for his lord, the Earl of Shrewsbury.

Have the characters make an Awareness + Ingenuity roll (Difficulty 15). Those who make it notice that he glances up at an upper room of the house when he says "special task." Someone is gazing down from the window. Characters who make an Awareness + Knowledge (History) roll (Difficulty 15) recall that, during Elizabeth's reign, the Earl of Shrewsbury was tasked with being the Keeper of Mary Stuart.

Sir Aldric takes the characters inside to the Baron's court, a large room with a desk and long table. Sir Aldric gestures them forward toward the Baron, who is sitting at one end of the table. Even seated the characters can tell that the Baron is a short man who hasn't missed many meals. A couple of servants bring wine and fruit to the table as the Baron examines them; he seems rather nervous as he speaks.

"Welcome. I am Lord Percival Rudwick, Baron of Mortenbury. Please sit and enjoy my table. Normally I wouldn't be quite so hospitable, but as the plague has found its way inside my walls I have extra fruit and wine to share. I'm certain that Sir Aldric has informed you that I could certainly use the services of good physicians.

"So, pray tell, who are you and what brings you to my barony? I trust you aren't stealing bodies?"

Cautious players may be worried that the food and drink is poisoned, but it is not. With Cybermats

THE NORTHERN KNIGHTS

roaming about, the Cybermen have left food supplies alone. As if to make the point, Lord Percival chooses a rather plump apple and takes a bite.

As the conversation progresses, the Baron shares the following information:

- The plague started about a week ago, just after a shooting star lit up the sky. Robert the Quack called it a sign, especially after a second, smaller star seemed to shoot up from the woods a few hours later. Local vicar the Reverend Godfrey Simpson called Robert's claim "witchcraft" and was one of the first to fall ill.
- Robert the Quack is a travelling healer who is always peddling cures and horoscopes. He's popular amongst the villagers due to his charm, but Lord Percival never considered him legitimate. The Constable, Hugo Bright, arrested Robert on suspicion of having started the plague (especially considering what happened to the vicar), but the healer maintained his innocence. The Constable soon fell ill too and the villagers almost killed Robert, but Lord Percival sent Sir Aldric to rescue him. Robert now rests safe within the castle and is currently tending to the fallen soldiers.

- As resilient as this plague seems, it has caused surprisingly few deaths. There are, however, rumours of body snatching going on, especially in homes with only a single ill patient. The Baron believes that these victims have actually been burned or buried discreetly by panicked neighbours.

- There's news along the northern border with Hawksfordshire that a secret army is gathering. If so, Lord Percival is certain that his castle is the target. He's sent word to the Earl and surrounding barons for assistance.
- Once the players realise that Mary is a 'guest' here, Lord Percival says that he dare not move her due to the plague, as he fears Elizabeth's wrath that much more if something happens to her. He has full faith in Sir Aldric to keep her safe within the castle walls of Mortenbury.
- The group is granted sanctuary within Mortenbury and the Baron prays that they'll be able to purge the plague from the castle. He also assigns them servants to take them to their rooms and get them properly attired for tonight's dinner.

LORD PERCIVAL RUDWICK, BARON OF MORTENBURY

AWARENESS	3	PRESENCE	3
COORDINATION	3	RESOLVE	2
INGENUITY	3	STRENGTH	2

Usually, Lord Percival is a jovial and entertaining host. His rather rotund figure (combined with his short height) indicates a comfortable life, although he is currently wracked with worry. When nervous he constantly fidgets and paces about, and as his body is out of shape he is constantly sweating.

Lord Percival is so worried about an attack that he's already sent his wife and children away to be with relatives in 'safer' lands.

SKILLS
Convince 2, Fighting 2, Knowledge 2, Marksman 1, Science 1, Technology 1, Transport 3.

TRAITS
Cowardly: Although he does his best to hide it, Lord Percival is a coward at heart. He lets Sir Aldric handle all of the martial decisions in the castle.
Obligation (Major): Lord Percival has a duty to his Earl and his Queen. Failure to live up to that duty can have dire consequences.

TECH LEVEL: 3   **STORY POINTS:** 6

A ROYAL REQUEST

This part of the scene can take place at an appropriate time during the group's conversation with the Baron. Mary Seton, Mary's lady-in-waiting, arrives to request the Queen's presence at dinner.

The door opens as the characters converse with the Baron. A well-dressed lady with a noble bearing enters the room and curtseys. The Baron wastes little time in addressing her.

"Lady Seton?"

The young woman smiles. "Her Majesty requests your presence at dinner this evening."

MARY SETON

AWARENESS	3	PRESENCE	3
COORDINATION	3	RESOLVE	4
INGENUITY	3	STRENGTH	1

Mary Seton is Mary's chief lady-in-waiting in Mortenbury Castle and her only contact with the rest of the world. She is a tall young woman in her late twenties with long red hair who carries herself like an aristocrat, being the daughter of a Scottish noble and a Frenchwoman who was a lady-in-waiting to Mary of Guise. She was educated with Mary in France and speaks French fluently (her accent is more French than Scottish). She has a bit of a crush on Sir Aldric and she and the Queen make a game of flirting with and teasing him. Unfortunately, this has backfired on Mary, as Sir Aldric is now smitten with the Queen.

SKILLS
Athletics 1, Convince 2, Craft 3, Knowledge 1, Medicine 1, Subterfuge 3, Survival 2, Transport 2.

TRAITS
Attractive: Mary gets a +2 bonus on rolls involving her looks.
Brave: Mary sticks by her mistress through the worst of times. She gets a +2 on Resolve rolls when she needs to show courage.
Obligation: Mary is loyal to her mistress and won't knowingly betray her.
Screamer! Mary has an ear-splitting scream that alert others to her dangers.

TECH LEVEL: 3   STORY POINTS: 4

The Baron chuckles. "You mean she wishes to join us at the table to meet the newcomers." He sips his wine as he glances around the table. Sir Aldric enthusiastically nods when the Baron looks at him. "Very well. I'm sure our guests would be honoured."

With a grateful nod and another curtsey the Lady in waiting leaves the room.

Characters watching her leave notice with an Awareness + Ingenuity roll (Difficulty 12) that Lady Seton obviously favours Sir Aldric. He barely acknowledges her in return.

SETTLING IN

At this point, the Baron has Sir Aldric and some servants escort the characters and Gabriel to their rooms to prepare for dinner. Gabriel requests that he be allowed to examine the sick guards. Other characters may join him but the Baron warns that dinner will be served in an hour and "the Queen doesn't like to be kept waiting." The Baron also offers the characters more appropriate attire to make them more presentable at dinner (giving them an opportunity to 'dress period').

⚙ 2. A NIGHT AT THE MORTENBURY

How this scene progresses depends on the character's actions for the evening. Some characters may choose to join Gabriel in visiting the soldiers, while others may wish to inspect the castle's defences (as it seems obvious a siege is coming), still others may wish to venture out to Mortenbury Village to see if they can find the body snatchers.

THE GARRISON

The Guard Barracks have been divided into two sections between sick soldiers and well soldiers, but the well barracks are empty. Currently, there are 22 ill soldiers in it, with servants running between them offering water and bread. Robert the Quack is here too, offering consolations and the occasional poultice to the ailing soldiers.

Characters who make an Awareness + Medicine roll (Difficulty 9 if they've seen the symptoms before, 15 if they have not) can confirm that these soldiers are afflicted with a fever and iron poisoning, amongst other symptoms. At this point (and especially if the characters spotted clues in the village), some characters may be looking for traces of disease carriers. One clue is in the thatched roof; a character making an Awareness + Subterfuge roll (Difficulty

15) notices that there are recent burn holes in the roof that did not start a fire (the Cybermats burrowed their way in after scaling the wall). If any of the soldiers on duty are questioned, one or two of them recall seeing something silver scurrying up the wall, but they assumed it was a rat (albeit a silver rat...) .

MORTENBURY CASTLE

The characters spend a great deal of time during this adventure in Mortenbury Castle (and possibly Hawksford Castle) as well. As the **Doctor Who Roleplaying Game** is a dramatic game it isn't necessary to go into great detail about every room in the castle. However, it helps to have some idea of where things are as the characters explore or defend the castle at various points during the adventure.

The castle sits just north of the city on a slight hill. The rear of the castle is protected by the River Bevern, while the rest of the castle is protected by two walls. Mortenbury Castle is relatively small, but a favourite of the Earl's for its good hunting in the nearby Mortenbury Forest.

Outer Wall: The first wall sits outside the hill and surrounds the castle except by the river, where it merges with the second wall. The gatehouse is built into this wall, as are several towers. Most of the guards are stationed along this wall but can quickly fall back if the wall is breached.

Bailey: This is the field between the two walls. It is effectively an island, as a second moat cuts between it and the hill (this moat joins the first through small holes in the outer wall beneath the water). The garrison and most of the servants are quartered here as well as the stables. During safer times the bailey is used as a marketplace, but given the importance of the Baron's guest, the plague and an impending threat, Lord Percival has closed the castle.

Inner Wall: This wall surrounds the main part of the castle and is where the guards fall back if the outer wall is breached. The inner wall boasts six cannons, although Lord Percival's garrison can generally only muster two or three at a time.

Courtyard: This small courtyard serves the Baron's family and guests as well as a private practice area for knights. It is surrounded on three sides by the Baron's house.

House: This is where the Baron, his family, knights (Sir Aldric is currently the only one) and most needed servants live. The great hall is rarely used except when the Earl is in residence; the Baron prefers to conduct business in his smaller counsel chamber.

Watchtower: Built atop the Inner Wall overlooking the river, the watchtower is the highest point of the castle and can see as far as the southern part of Hawksfordshire. At least one soldier mans this post at all times.

Dungeon: The dungeon sits beneath the house and courtyard, although it is actually at sea level. The rear of the dungeon, facing the river, hosts four smaller cannons that are used to fend off river assaults. Only the river-facing end of the dungeon is exposed, as the rest of the dungeon is covered with the earth of the hill.

Ever since a proper jail was built in Mortenbury, the Baron's dungeon has rarely seen prisoners and is more properly used for storage. It also contains a secret tunnel out of the castle and into the wood a little over a half kilometre away.

ROBERT THE QUACK

Robert is an itinerant healer that travels from village to village to hawk his herbal remedies. He is also keen to learn how to transmute minerals to gold, but this has thus far eluded him. Robert is a tall, lanky man approaching 40, with thinning black hair and a thick beard. He dresses garishly and always has at least a few charms and poultices about his person. He claims to have studied under John Dee (actually, he's visited Dee's library but has only spoken with the noted mathematician on a couple of occasions).

Robert is a man stuck between two worlds: magic and science. While he correctly believes that there is wisdom in the old ways (especially herbalism), Robert puts just as much faith in more dubious magical practices and superstitions. He also practices astrology and alchemy in curious blends of magical theory and scientific experimentation. In short, he is like most other scientists of the Elizabethan era.

While his 'cures' are rarely helpful, what Robert excels at is making his patients feel better. If the characters encounter him with the sick soldiers, they find him cheering them up and raising their spirits even as they shiver through their pain. Unfortunately only a handful can take advantage of his entertaining manner, as most have fallen into feverish comas.

If the characters speak to Robert he'll pretend that his cures are working but if he loses an opposed Resolve + Convince roll then he'll admit defeat. He's doing the best he can to make the soldiers comfortable but he's honestly stumped as to the nature of the plague. He thought he'd contracted it just before he was arrested, but he showed no signs other than a mild cold while incarcerated.

Robert has heard that people are disappearing in Mortenbury. He's even heard rumours of plague victims being snatched in the dead of night. Unfortunately, unaffected villagers are too scared to go from house to house to see who's missing, so some of these sightings of body snatchers are unsubstantiated.

While a showman first and foremost, Robert does have a kind heart and is willing to aid the group in any way he can. If asked about the shooting star, Robert says that it was large and bright. He'd swear it fell in Hawkwood in Hawksfordshire, but he knows that's daft. Only if the characters seem open to the idea of a falling star will he reveal that he thought he saw a smaller star shoot up to the heavens soon after the falling star landed.

While Robert doesn't realise it, the many charms, herbs, minerals, poultices and tinctures that he keeps in his wagon (currently parked inside the bailey) contain elements for a brew that can clog and destroy a Cyberman's chest unit. This requires an hour's work and three successful Ingenuity + Science rolls (Difficulty 18). This is reduced to one successful roll if the character has the Biochemical Genius trait.

ROBERT THE QUACK

AWARENESS	3	PRESENCE	4
COORDINATION	2	RESOLVE	3
INGENUITY	4	STRENGTH	2

Robert the Quack is an itinerant peddler of cures and charms.

SKILLS
Athletics 2, Convince 4, Craft 3, Fighting 2, Knowledge 3, Marksman 1, Medicine 4, Science 4, Subterfuge 3, Survival 2, Technology 2, Transport 2.

TRAITS
Charming: A consummate showman, Robert has a magnetic personality and gains +2 on rolls to impress or persuade people.
Resourceful Pockets: Robert always seems to have something beneficial on his person – or in his wagon – when he needs it. He can either spend a Story Point to have something useful or roll two dice. He finds the useful item if he rolls any double.

TECH LEVEL: 3   STORY POINTS: 4

Robert the Quack provides characters with a couple of different opportunities, which they may be able to exploit now or later:

The Coffee Cure: Robert the Quack had contracted the plague during the initial Cybermat attack. Anyone examining Robert and making an Awareness + Medicine roll (Difficulty 9) shows the healing marks of a Cybermat bite on the back of his shoulder. If asked, Robert recalls waking up the morning that he was arrested feeling hot; his shoulder felt a little itchy and stiff as well. Nevertheless he got up and made himself a pot of coffee and a fried egg.

Characters making an Awareness + Knowledge (History) roll (Difficulty 15) recall that coffee has

THE NORTHERN KNIGHTS

barely made its way to England at this time and it's likely that Robert the Quack is the only person in the area with some on hand. If the characters can convince or coerce Robert to part with his small bag of coffee, then they can brew enough to get the garrison back on its feet.

Chemical Laboratory: Characters who decide to investigate Robert's wagon (or who go to retrieve the coffee from it) note that Robert has a lot of useful ingredients for various chemical and pharmaceutical concoctions, including many of which Robert isn't even aware. This will become important later as the characters try to brainstorm ways to beat the Cybermen.

MEETING THE QUEEN

As is customary, the host and guests are seated according to station. Lord Percival has decided to humour Mary by allowing her to be seated first, Lady Mary Seton along with her. Lord Percival enters with the characters, apologising for his family's non-attendance (as he sent them away when the plague started). Sir Aldric is also in attendance

and perceptive characters may notice flirty glances exchanged between him and the exiled Queen.

The meal starts with a mutton pottage and bread followed by boiled pork loin and vegetables. The meal is finished with a cheesecake. During the meal Lord Percival asks how the defences are; Sir Aldric confidently states that the defences will hold, so long as no one else succumbs to the plague.

MARY STUART, QUEEN OF SCOTS

AWARENESS	4	PRESENCE	5
COORDINATION	3	RESOLVE	4
INGENUITY	3	STRENGTH	2

Now in her early thirties, Mary is beginning the transition from beautiful young woman to haggard prisoner. She is still in the early stages so she is still very attractive and her little game with Mary Seton over Sir Aldric's affections has spurred her to maintain herself, but more melancholic (and unadorned) moments reveal a face perhaps a decade older than it should be. While a Scottish aristocrat in England, Mary still prefers to converse in French and has Continental manners. She spends a lot of time writing letters to supporters, although she is (thus far) careful not to incriminate herself in any way.

Whether Mary is really in league with the recusants or something of an innocent victim is up to the Gamemaster and should be played accordingly. History is seldom writ in stone and it's quite possible that the Mary that the characters meet is quite different from the one they learned

about in school. If Mary wants to be rescued, she'll certainly do what she can to aid in her escape. If she is simply a victim of circumstance, than she'll likely want to remain with the Baron rather than risk Elizabeth's vengeance.

SKILLS

Convince 4, Craft 3, Knowledge 3, Marksman 1, Science 2, Subterfuge 3, Survival 1, Transport 2.

TRAITS

Attractive: Mary is quite beautiful and gains a +2 on rolls in which her appearance would play a role.

Charming: Mary gets a +2 on rolls when she turns on the charm.

Linguist: Mary knows several European languages, including English, French, Greek, Latin and Spanish.

Selfish: Mary's designs on the English throne and her affinity with France have often caused her to choose imprudent courses of action which have led to her current imprisonment.

TECH LEVEL: 3   STORY POINTS: 6

Should it come to that, Lord Percival asks the characters if any of them can fight. For her part, Mary seems to take it all in stride, as a bit of mystery and excitement is a welcome diversion. She asks the characters about their backgrounds and how they came to be here.

This dinner is a good opportunity to establish the abdicated queen's personality and her association with other members of the Baron's household (see **Mary Stuart, Queen of Scots** for advice on how to portray her).

Have the characters make Awareness + Ingenuity rolls (Difficulty 18). Anyone that succeeds realises that, like the Marys, Gabriel seems to take an interest in Sir Aldric, especially as the dinner goes on. He's been noticing the flirty glances that the knight has been exchanging with the Queen and he's wondering, as Walsingham's agent, whether Sir Aldric might be aiding the effort to free Mary.

After dinner Lord Percival asks Sir Aldric to increase the night watch, as he fears for an attack. Sir Aldric notes that it will be tough, but he'll ensure that the guards are strengthened for an early morning attack, as Lord Tristan, the most likely candidate, wouldn't dare march at night. Gabriel seems especially concerned that castle security is left in Sir Aldric's hands, but he says nothing.

BODY SNATCHERS

While the characters are warned not to venture out of the castle at night, Lord Percival won't stop them from leaving. It's raining fairly hard this evening so the characters will need to bundle up unless they want to get wet.

Unfortunately, they may find themselves beset upon in the town by night watchmen, unless one or more of them are wearing a physician's field outfit. The night watchmen are a hastily organised group of townsfolk who are on the lookout for body snatchers.

Since some of those snatched lived alone and were last visited by a physician, the night watchmen view all physicians as suspects. But they've also been somewhat intimidated by a physician recently, so keep their distance from a physician when they meet one (see below).

The true culprit is a Cyberman disguised as a physician. This Cyberman is somewhat intimidating so the night watchmen are scared to approach him. The Cyberman enters homes to check on victims, but is smart enough to mind control only those victims he has not visited that evening (often by walking past the house). This victim then gets up after several minutes and 'sleepwalks' to a designated point, where the collectors are waiting for them.

The collectors are the Earl of Hawksford's men mind controlled by the Cybermen to collect the people coming to them and carry them back to Hawksford Castle to await conversion.

The Physician Bogeyman: The Cybermen have scared off most of the night watchmen, with the end result that they keep their distance from any physician they meet. This allows the Cybermen to continue their work unmolested.

A perceptive character making an Awareness + Presence roll (the Empathy trait bonus counts) (Difficulty 15) notes that the night watchmen seem scared if any of them are dressed as a physician.

Sleepwalker: At some point after midnight, one of the plague victims gets out of bed and walks out of his or her house. The victim is easily identifiable as wearing bedclothes and can be followed north-east, toward the upper edge of Mortenbury Forest, near the border with Hawksfordshire. A cart is waiting for them here, along with two farmers from Hawksfordshire.

Both the victim and the farmers are being mind controlled by the Cybermen. The Cybermen are using a more primitive technique than the EarPods they've used in the past, instead using a combination of elevated iron and sulphur levels in the victim's bloodstream with magnetic fields. If the mind control is broken then they collapse into a fevered heap.

If the farmers' hypnosis is broken then they'll have no idea how they got this far south and beg to be allowed to return home. Unfortunately, they'll probably be threatening the characters long before that, as they are programmed to kill anyone who learns of their presence (see opposite for their stats).

Physicians: Gabriel isn't the only physician in the village. A few others mill about and can give the characters information about strange-acting night watchmen or somewhat bulky, silent physicians in field dress. This is a good encounter if you want to slip clues to the players that they might have missed.

Cyberman Physician: If you really want to surprise the players (especially if they've already identified the Cybermats), then you can bring them face to face with the Cyberman masquerading as a physician. The lumbering giant slowly makes the rounds, speaking in a somewhat monotone voice only when necessary.

The Cyberman attempts to warn off the characters with his stun weapon, but if they persist he'll resort to lethal force. He'll want to take anyone that reveals themselves to be a time traveller back to the Scout Ship, preferably having rendered them.

The Cyberman physician takes the direct route back to Hawkwood; he won't seek out the Collectors first. It's not in his interest to be tied to them or the sleepwalking plague victims.

COLLECTOR

AWARENESS	4	PRESENCE	2
COORDINATION	3	RESOLVE	2
INGENUITY	2	STRENGTH	3

The Collectors are mind-controlled farmers that are working for the Cybermen. They've been trained to cover their tracks with brute force, but if they are freed from their hypnotised state then they'll remember nothing other than receiving a visit from the Earl and his strangely armoured knights.

SKILLS
Athletics 2, Craft 3, Fighting 3, Marksman 3, Medicine 1, Science 1, Survival 3, Transport 2.

EQUIPMENT: Crossbow (4), a variety of axes and bladed weapons (+2 Strength in combat).

TECH LEVEL: 3   STORY POINTS: 3

NIGHT WATCHMAN

AWARENESS	3	PRESENCE	2
COORDINATION	2	RESOLVE	2
INGENUITY	2	STRENGTH	3

Far from an elite police force, the night watchmen are largely middle-aged shopkeepers and craftsmen that shout the time (usually inaccurately) and call for aid if they see a crime. They are ill-equipped for combat, but do surprisingly well in large numbers.

The Cyberman 'physician' has scared many of these night watchmen sufficiently that they will look the other way when any physician approaches. If quizzed about this, they won't really know what was so scary about the 'physician', just that there was something unnatural about him.

SKILLS
Athletics 1, Fighting 2, Marksman 1, Subterfuge 2, Survival 1, Transport 2.

TRAITS
The night watchmen have a variety of traits. Some are physically impaired, some are especially brave and some might be argumentative to a fault. The Gamemaster should feel free to improvise as necessary.

EQUIPMENT: Cudgel, lantern.

TECH LEVEL: 3   **STORY POINTS:** 2

CYBERMAT ATTACK

The characters may very well have met the Cybermen before and might correctly guess that the plague is the result of Cybermat activity. The Cybermats travel through the River Bevern and crawl up the side of the castle facing the river, which is not a place that the soldiers would think to keep an eye on (at least not unless they hear a lot of noise).

The Cybermats are being sent to the castle one last time this evening to soften up the garrison for an attack at dawn. This attack only commences if the Cybermats are successful. If the characters find a way to defeat the Cybermats then Lord Tristan and the Cybermen will be forced to use a subtler approach. Defeating the Cybermats requires some creativity as the characters are in a low-tech time period.

The Cybermats attack just after midnight. There are four of them, enough to quickly infect half or more of the remaining garrison before they slink away.

- **Isolating the Garrison:** One way for the characters to thwart the Cybermats is to insist that sleeping soldiers congregate in a sealed room, or at least one in which the opening can be carefully guarded. In spite of the Cybermats' corrosive powers they can't bore through stone (at least, not quickly enough), so spiriting the soldiers away in one of the castle's inner rooms should do the trick.

- **Cocktail Robert:** Administering a corrosive or sticky chemical mixture will destroy a Cybermat. The characters need access to many chemicals (fortunately Robert has an ample supply if they can convince him to help). An Ingenuity + Science roll (Difficulty 18, reduced to 12 if the character has the Biochemical Genius trait) is necessary to concoct a 'cocktail' that, when thrown at a Cybermat or a Cybermat is immersed in, will slow down and/or destroy it.

- **Electrocution:** While an Elizabethan castle doesn't have electrical power, it does have a lot of conductive metals that they might be able to electrify with an anachronistic bit of technology they might have on them. A character could bang out the metal and wait for a Cybermat to crawl over it. Once the Cybermat is on the metal the character electrifies it (water can be used for the same purpose).

The character needs something with which to electrify it. This may be supplied by something with a battery in the character's possession. Alternatively, as it is raining, a character could rig up a lightning rod to attract lightning. This would require the expenditure of a few story points.

- **Robert Blend Coffee:** If the characters have already discovered that coffee can fight off this plague then administering coffee to the newly infected helps them break the fever quicker. As with the other soldiers, two-thirds of the newly infected are able to muster their strength to defend the castle by mid-morning and the rest in the afternoon.

- **Protecting Minds from Hypnosis:** The characters might have encountered mind-controlling Cybermen before – the Doctor certainly has, if he's present. Alternatively, a Boffin might be able to use Jiggery-Pokery to rig some sort of Mind Guard. Finding a circuit in Elizabethan England could be a problem, however; unless the characters are willing to destroy a technological item in their possession then it takes 2 Story Points for the first circuit and 1 Story Point for each additional circuit (these may be in the TARDIS, inside an unnecessary piece of personal equipment). Or they could take a Cybermat apart for spares...

THE AGENT

Dr Gabriel Field uses this opportunity to see how well guarded Mary is and whether she's part of a Catholic plot. His activities require him to sneak around the castle, attempt to intercept letters to or from Mary, check the layout of the castle for potential escape routes; in other words, exactly the sorts of things that should make players suspicious of his activities.

CYBERMAT

AWARENESS	4	PRESENCE	1
COORDINATION	4	RESOLVE	5
INGENUITY	2	STRENGTH	5*

Cybermats are small, cybernetic creatures used as vanguards, scouts and energy thieves by the Cybermen. They resemble a large silver insect or – from a distance – a rat. Beneath their metallic shell they have a real mouth taken from one of the Cybermen's victims. They have a rudimentary intelligence, and can 'play dead' to escape notice or fool their prey. They can be stunned by a zap from a Sonic Screwdriver, and a strong burst of electricity will scramble their brains.

*A Cybermat's Strength is for pushing or pulling only. Similarly, a Cybermat only does as programmed; its Technology and Transport skills are only for seeking out the proper wiring or circuitry to corrode and destroy equipment or gadgets.

SKILLS

Athletics 5, Fighting 2, Marksman 4, Subterfuge 5, Survival 2, Technology 3*, Transport 3*.

TRAITS

Alien Appearance: Cybermats look like large metallic insects or rats.
Alien Senses: A Cybermat has a number of senses, including infrared and ultraviolet vision. It also has the ability to home in on human brainwaves.
Armour (Minor): The Cybermats' metallic armour reduces damage by 5. Cybermats are particularly susceptible to electric charges; their armour does not count against an electric charge.
Clinging: The Cybermat can climb even smooth surfaces without difficulty.
Cyborg: While it looks like a small robot, a Cybermat is a partially organic creature like the Cybermen themselves.

Enslaved: The Cybermats are the servants of the Cybermen.
Environmental (Major): Cybermats can survive underwater and in the vacuum of space.
Jumping: A Cybermat's advanced hydraulics enable it to leap 5-6 feet in the air, perfect for landing on a humanoid's back or shoulder. By spending a Story Point, the Cybermat can automatically take an unsuspecting foe by surprise with this attack.
Natural Weapon (Bite): A Cybermat can bite an opponent, inflicting (1/3/4) levels of damage. Their bite contains a corrosive or poison, as described on pg. 31.
Natural Weapon (Electric Discharge): Cybermats have the ability to discharge electricity at close range, delivering either Stun (S/S/S) or Lethal (4/L/L) damage.
Weakness (Major): Cybermats have the same major weaknesses as their masters, such as solvents, liquid plastic and radiation. A solvent is more difficult to administer to a Cybermat as it has to go through the mouth. They are also susceptible to electric charges (see above).

TECH LEVEL: 7   STORY POINTS: 1-2

This proves especially interesting if you go with the **Star-Crossed Lovers** option too.

Gabriel searches Sir Aldric's room while he's elsewhere too, hoping to find some evidence against him. Gabriel does find a letter that Sir Aldric is writing to a "Laird Dougal McKendra," a known supporter of Mary. Sir Aldric has crossed out part of the letter and apparently intended to discard it but it is written "on behalf of Queen Mary and our previous association, whom I pray I can count on your discretion and support in a very dear matter."

In truth, Mary has been terribly missing a favourite brooch that she'd entrusted to the Laird's wife and Sir Aldric hopes to get it for her. His intentions are purely romantic; as it happens his cousin does regular business with the Laird in textiles. In the hands of a Walsingham zealot, such as Gabriel, this letter is damning proof of his association.

As Gabriel noted Mary Seton's attitude towards Sir Aldric, he may try to gain her trust himself. He flirts with her a bit and casually mentions that he is going to Hawksfordshire as soon as he is able. Gabriel hopes that Mary Stuart will try to send correspondence through him that he can turn over to Walsingham for study. In a bit of turnabout, these actions may make Sir Aldric as suspicious of Gabriel as Gabriel is of him.

⚙ 3. THE SILVER EMISSARY

While this scene starts with the possibility of battle, it is quickly defused when Lord Percival's garrison turns out to be stronger than Lord Tristan had hoped. The Cybermen offer terms, but the players know better. They'll have to stop the Cybermen from taking Mary and then take the battle to them.

ENEMY SIGHTED!

At dawn, the soldier in the watchtower sights a small army marching into Shropshire from Hawksfordshire. This news is hastily shared with the Baron, who orders Sir Aldric to prepare the defences. This can be quite a tense situation if the garrison was knocked down by half again by Cybermats.

Lord Percival calls Gabriel and the characters to his counsel chamber and grants them the option of fleeing while they can. Sieges are nasty affairs and it's likely that the plague will only further take hold; he won't hold it against them for leaving. Of course, he's more than happy to have their assistance as well. There is a light rain today and Sir Aldric prays

it means that gunpowder won't shatter the walls any time soon.

If the characters used 'Cocktail Robert' against the Cybermats then they might want to consider making another batch, especially if they know that Cybermen are about (see **Cocktail Robert, Redux** below). Sir Aldric may even suggest attaching the mixture to arrowheads and crossbow bolts (although he considers this all witchcraft, he's a practical man).

ELIZABETHAN WEAPONRY

For convenience's sake there are only four types of Elizabethan firearm used in this adventure:

Arquebus: The standard soldier's rifle. 2/5/7

Belt Pistol: Pistols are rare and expensive. In this adventure only the Lords carry them. 2/4/6

Cannon: Cannons come in several sizes, although the size doesn't matter much if a cannonball hits you. 4/L/L

Musket: A heavier rifle; the musket is designed to pierce armour. 3/7/10

REINFORCEMENTS

If the characters administered the coffee to the sick garrison members then they'll notice a marked improvement in the morning. Two-thirds of the infected soldiers are already out of bed. They still have runny noses but their strength and clarity is back. The fevers are beginning to break on the rest and they'll be ready to fight by the afternoon. The characters and Robert are heartily congratulated by both Lord Percival and Sir Aldric.

If the characters have not, then Lord Percival (or the characters) must spend 5 Story Points for enough relief forces to arrive to replace the sick soldiers. This is an advance guard sent by the Earl, who should be here himself the next morning with a small army. The Baron need only hold out for one day.

In either case Sir Aldric sends some soldiers into Mortenbury to bring the citizens, both sick and plague-ridden, into the Bailey. If Lord Tristan is this bold then it's too dangerous for innocents to be left in his path. The characters can aid in the evacuation if they wish; Gabriel helps as well so long as he is still trusted (see **The Agent**, above).

Sir Aldric orders the cannons prepared and has the soldiers load their firearms and longbows. Lord Percival orders Mary Stuart to the dungeon where she can be quickly be spirited away through the tunnel if necessary.

THE SIEGE

Lord Tristan manoeuvres his troops around the castle, but he does not like what he sees. Mortenbury's garrison is almost at full capacity. He asks the Silver Knight (the leader of the Cybermen) how this is possible and the Silver Knight decides to go with Plan B. He holds up a white flag and rides toward the castle drawbridge.

Plan B essentially boils down to allowing Lord Percival to lower his guard as two other Cybermen enter the castle via the secret tunnel. They plan to 'rescue' the Queen by any means necessary. As a potential tip-off to this plan, Sir Aldric spots a servant standing next to the mounted Lord Tristan. The servant, Molly Waters, had contracted the disease several days ago and was supposedly still locked up somewhere in the castle (in reality she sleepwalked off and now, mind controlled by the Cybermen, is giving Lord Tristan valuable intelligence about the castle's layout.

A character making an Awareness + Ingenuity roll (Difficulty 15) is able to make out a description of the servant advising Lord Tristan; Sir Aldric, Lord Percival, or any member of Mortenbury Castle should be able to identify Molly based on the description (young woman, pretty face, long curly strawberry-blonde hair).

ENGLISH SOLDIERS

AWARENESS	3	PRESENCE	2
COORDINATION	3	RESOLVE	3
INGENUITY	2	STRENGTH	4

SKILLS
Athletics 3, Convince 1, Craft 1, Fighting 3, Knowledge 1, Marksman 3, Medicine 1, Subterfuge 2, Survival 3, Transport 3.

EQUIPMENT: Armour (8 torso only), various weapons.

TECH LEVEL: 3   **STORY POINTS:** 2

LORD TRISTAN STEELE, EARL OF HAWKSFORD

AWARENESS	3	PRESENCE	5
COORDINATION	4	RESOLVE	3
INGENUITY	3	STRENGTH	7

Lord Tristan Steele lives up to his surname; it is said that he has a heart of steel although his soul is devout. He genuinely believes that the arrival of the Cybermen is Divine Providence. He wishes not only to free Mary but to marry her, making him King of England. Lord Tristan has been partially Cyber-converted, but he still has a fully human head. He still needs to eat and breathe normally (although the amount of food is minimal, and alcohol no longer affects him) and he is unaffected by chemical cocktails (or gold dust) as he has no respiration grille.

SKILLS
Athletics 4, Convince 4, Craft 1, Fighting 4, Knowledge 2, Marksman 4, Subterfuge 3, Survival 3, Technology 1, Transport 2.

TRAITS
Armour: Lord Tristan has a Cyberman's body, granting him 10 points of protection. This protection does not cover his head.
Cyborg: Lord Tristan has availed himself of the benefits of being friends with the Cybermen. He is now a Cyberman from the neck down.
Dark Secret: Well, it's hardly a secret for long, but Lord Tristan's allies are Cybermen and his partial-conversion has sent him a little loopy.
Obligation (Major): Lord Tristan is an English Peer and obligated to uphold the laws of the realm, in spite of his recusant status.
Obsession (Minor): Lord Tristan believes in the Catholic cause and does whatever he can to support it.
Voice of Authority: As far as most of the locals are concerned, Lord Tristan is the authority. He receives a +2 bonus to Presence or Convince rolls when exercising it.

EQUIPMENT: Belt Pistol (2/4/6), Rapier (+2 Strength), Knife.

TECH LEVEL: 3   **STORY POINTS:** 10

- **Securing the Tunnel:** Characters who hear about the 'turncoat' servants may guess that the escape tunnel has been compromised. Worse, Lord Percival has sent Mary down to the dungeon in case they need the tunnel, which makes the Cybermen's rescue attempt that much easier. characters that rush down to the dungeon at this point can get there in plenty of time before the Cybermen (and their altered servant). They might consider a way to plug the tunnel or at least get Mary somewhere safer. They may bump into Gabriel at this point, which may spark a conflict as Gabriel wants her to be rescued (at least long enough for him to justify killing her).

- **Cocktail Robert, Redux:** Once again, the characters can whip up a chemical cocktail that wreaks havoc with a Cyberman's chest unit. Unfortunately, the mix needs to be slightly stickier than those used for Cybermats, requiring three successful Ingenuity + Science roll (Difficulty 18), reduced to just one roll for those with Biochemical Genius. The chemical cocktail needs to be smashed against the chest unit in order to be effective.

GOLD?

If you've decided that gold is useful against these Cybermen then it's readily available, especially in a lord's home. The more difficult task is getting Baron Mortenbury to part with the odd gold candelabra or coin.

WHITE FLAG

The Silver Knight rides toward the castle, hoisting a white flag. Lord Percival tells Sir Aldric to allow the Silver Knight to enter the bailey to negotiate, as he wants Lord Tristan to know how well protected Mortenbury Castle is to dissuade him from attacking. Mortenbury soldiers lower the gate and allow the Knight entry. It soon seems a mistake (if the characters have never met a Cyberman then emphasise the obviously alien nature of the armour and horse).

As the silver-armoured rider enters the gate he is met with fear and dread. He is riding a beast that seems from the depths of hell, a silver-armoured steed with glowing red eyes and steam shooting from its nostrils. To the soldiers of Mortenbury the knight wears strange armour, clad from head to toe in smooth, silver metal. He grips the flagpole with a gauntlet. In place of a tabard or colours the knight wears a giant amulet upon his chest, and his helmet resembles an actor's mask with no nose and strange hand-grips on either side.

To time travellers, of course, the Silver Knight's appearance isn't curious at all. He is a Cyberman!

This revelation will be quite a shock to players who have missed the clues thus far, but for most it'll just be confirmation of what they've already pieced together. What they don't know is why the Cybermen are working with Lord Tristan and what the Cyberman hopes to gain through parley.

In the meantime, Lord Percival gathers his admittedly low courage and bellows at the Cyberman from his perch above the inner wall gate.

"I know you not, Silver Knight," the Lord of the Castle declares. "It would seem that Lord Tristan is reduced to hiring mercenaries to commit his treason for him. What are your terms, Sir Knight?"

The Silver Knight looks up at Lord Percival. When he speaks, the reverberation in his voice causes everyone around him to step back. It is as if the Devil himself speaks.

"You know the terms, Baron Mortenbury. Surrender the Queen of Scotland and your lives will be spared."

Lord Percival laughs nervously.

"Look around you, Sir Knight. This castle is well defended and the Earl's army is on its way. You won't be able to penetrate our walls before reinforcements arrive."

The Silver Knight remains silent for a few moments. His hellish steed grunts another puff of steam. For a second, it looks as if the Silver Knight would turn and ride out, beaten in the parley. Alas, that is not to be. Instead, the Silver Knight speaks in his infernal voice once more.

"Penetrating your walls is not necessary."

Lord Percival's eyes widen. "A siege, then? We can certainly hold out a day, and much more than that if necessary."

"No," the Silver Knight corrects him. "You misunderstand. It is not necessary to penetrate the walls because we are already inside them."

CYBERMEN

AWARENESS	2	PRESENCE	3
COORDINATION	2	RESOLVE	3
INGENUITY	2	STRENGTH	7

Lord Tristan's strange allies are Cybermen. Their leader is referred to by Lord Tristan as "the Silver Knight." To further the theme of knighthood, the Cybermen have taken to wearing swords and carrying shields, and they have converted horses to act as mounts, but they're hardly in disguise.

SKILLS
Convince 2, Fighting 3, Marksman 2, Medicine 1, Science 1, Technology 4, Transport 2.

TRAITS
Armour (Major): The Cybermen's metallic armour reduces damage by 10.
Cyborg: The Cybermen were once human, but have had everything but their major internal organs replaced with machinery.
Environmental (Major): Cybermen can survive underwater and in the vacuum of space.
Fear Factor (3): Cybermen are pretty scary and gain a +6 to rolls to actively scare someone.
Flight: Cybermen have rockets in their boots that allow them to fly at the same speed as a commercial airliner.
Natural Weapon – Particle Beam: Cybermen have arm-mounted particle beams (4/L/L).
Natural Weapon – Electric Grip: The Cyberman's grip delivers a powerful blast of electricity, increasing the damage in close combat to (4/9/13).
Networked: Cybermen are connected by wireless technology to a collective hive mind.
Possess (Special): These Cybermen are using magnetic fields to mind control humans that have elevated levels of iron and sulphur in their bloodstreams.

Slow
Special – Quicksilver: A Cyberman can move in short bursts of lightning speed, quicker than the human eye can follow. Each burst of speed costs 1 Story Point and gives the Cyberman a speed of 20 for one round.
Weakness (Major): The Cybermen's chest unit is particularly vulnerable to clogging or dissolving with chemical mixtures (e.g. 'Cocktail Polly'), liquid plastic and gold dust. They are also vulnerable to strong magnetic fields, awfully like those they're using to mind control the humans. If one of these can be turned on them, the Cyberman must make a Resolve + Strength roll (Difficulty 18). A Bad Result means the emotion inhibitor shuts down, driving the Cyberman crazy. A Disastrous Result destroys the Cyberman.

TECH LEVEL: 7   STORY POINTS: 1-2

THE NORTHERN KNIGHTS

The Cyberman's last sentence sends everyone in and around the bailey into a panic as they ready their weapons and glance about, as if Lord Tristan's forces are about to spring out of a building and pour into the bailey. Unless the characters stop him, the Cyberman turns and rides out the gate.

CYBER-STEED

AWARENESS	2	PRESENCE	1
COORDINATION	6	RESOLVE	4
INGENUITY	1	STRENGTH	7

A Cyber-steed is a horse that has undergone Cyber-conversion, resembling somewhat a Cyber-shade. Like the Cybermen, Cyber-steeds have steel-clad helmets and armoured chest units, as well as steel-shod hooves. The rest of the animal remains distinctly equine, however.

SKILLS
Athletics 5, Fighting 3, Marksman 3, Survival 3.

TRAITS
Alien Senses: A Cyber-steed has a number of senses, including infrared and ultraviolet vision.
Armour (Major Trait): The Cyber-steed's metallic armour reduces damage by 5.
Cyborg
Enslaved: Cyber-steeds are the servants of the Cybermen.
Jumping: Cyber-steeds can jump over obstacles that most horses can't reach. They get +2 to Strength and Athletics rolls when jumping.
Natural Weapon – Chest Beam: Cyber-steeds have a particle beam directly built into their chest units (4/L/L).
Natural Weapon – Stomp/Kick: Cyber-steeds can use their hydraulic legs to make a powerful kick or stomp (4/9/13).
Weakness (Major): The Cyber-steed's chest unit is particularly vulnerable to clogging or dissolving with chemical mixtures (e.g. 'Cocktail Polly') and liquid plastic. Due to their design Cyber-steed chest units can be 'choked' with gold dust.

STORY POINTS: 1-2

- **Testing Cocktail Robert:** While not very sporting, a character can test any chemical concoctions on the Silver Knight, as he is exposed and his chest unit can be easily hit by a well-placed arrow. No

one else will take the shot as the Silver Knight came under a flag of truce and Sir Aldric may even turn against the characters for such a 'cowardly' act. As soon as the Silver Knight is revealed to be something not quite human, however, the criticism is muted. If the characters act and miss then the Silver Knight uses his advanced weaponry to attack while relaying a message to his cohorts. The Cybermen remaining with Lord Tristan order him to attack.

- **Putting Two and Two Together:** Anyone listening to the Silver Knight may realise that there is one place that the castle can be infiltrated: the Secret Tunnel! If the characters act now, they can get to the tunnel before the Cybermen arrive. If not, you can allow them to spend a Story Point to realise this.

THE SIEGE
Once the Silver Knight leaves the castle, Lord Tristan presses his attack. This ends up being an intermittent exchange of gunfire (the rain makes it difficult for sustained fire) and the occasional arrow or bolt, as well as a belch or three from the garrison cannons.

Using information gained from Molly Waters, a new set of six Cybermats are sent out of the river and up the walls to wreak havoc on the garrison. Two of these Cybermats actually crawl inside the dungeon cannon holes in order to weaken the cannon crews there.

At this point, there are a number of different ways the characters might be able to help out:

- **Pest Control:** The characters are probably on the lookout for another wave of Cybermat attacks. If so then they can use similar tactics to the ones they used before – the Cybermats aren't smart enough to have adapted their tactics.

- **Sniper:** It may occur to a character that the Cybermen can be sniped with a missile containing Cocktail Robert, a 'gold glitter globe' or something similar. In addition to the small size of the target (the chest unit), the range and rain make such a shot difficult but not impossible (probably inflicting a penalty of -6 or even a -8).

It may also occur to a character that Lord Tristan is vulnerable as well. At this point in the adventure Lord Tristan uses his Story Points to survive a sniper attack and retreats into cover.

SO WHERE ARE THE PLAGUE VICTIMS?

Savvy players may wonder what the Cybermen are doing with the plague victims they've acquired, as there are only a few mind-controlled humans at the siege. The answer is obvious to those familiar with Cybermen; the Cybermen are building a new army back at their crashed spaceship.

DUNGEONS AND CYBERMEN

While the Silver Knight parleys with Lord Percival, two Cybermen and two mind-controlled humans have already entered the secret tunnel and are heading into the dungeon of the castle. Unfortunately, this is where Mary Stuart and her handmaiden Mary Seton are waiting to escape if it all goes wrong.

Gabriel is hiding in the shadows here, waiting for the Scottish Queen to either do something incriminating or get shot in the back while trying to escape. There are two soldiers stationed with the women but they're no match for Cybermen.

Assuming that the characters do not arrive in time (see above), the Cybermen and hypnotised humans emerge from the tunnel and startle the two Marys as well as the soldiers (and Gabriel). The soldiers attack while the women scream, alerting the cannon crews to their predicament. The Cybermen dispatch all would-be saviours with relative ease before grabbing Mary Stuart (they ignore Mary Seton) and exiting through the tunnel. At this point Gabriel rushes out, grabs an arquebus, shoots Mary in the back, and then plants the arquebus near one of the fallen soldiers.

If the players do arrive in time, here are some suggestions as to what they might do:

- **Collapsing the Tunnel:** Assuming that the characters get down to the dungeon in time, they may be able to collapse the tunnel before the Cybermen can use it to enter the castle. There's certainly enough gunpowder stored in barrels in the dungeon to use. This requires an Ingenuity + Technology roll (Difficulty 12) to blow up the tunnel (characters may act more dramatically by waiting for the Cybermen to approach before blowing the tunnel, catching them in the blast). Alternatively, a character with a suitably fancy weapon such as a laser can collapse the tunnel.

- **Electrifying the Tunnel Door:** A character can electrify the door in order to electrocute a Cyberman to death. This requires some Jiggery-Pokery, as the character has to cannibalise a piece of futuristic equipment (see pg. 40). This is considered a Minor Gadget. This only works once, as only the first Cyberman will be fooled into touching the door. The second uses his particle beam to destroy it.

- **Using the Cannon:** Since the secret tunnel is on the same level as the dungeon cannons, it's certainly possible to wheel a cannon around to face the tunnel door and attack anyone entering the tunnel (and potentially collapsing the tunnel as well).

- **Engaging the Cybermen:** Another way to fight the Cybermen is to attack them directly by either smashing Cocktail Robert (or something similar) into their chest units or using a futuristic weapon. This comes at great risk, as the Cybermen won't hesitate to use their particle beams and electric grips against any attackers.

- **Moving the Marys to Safety:** Rather than defeat the Cybermen the characters may opt to secure the Marys by moving them somewhere else. Gabriel follows them, looking for his opportunity.

- **Gabriel:** At this point, Gabriel is looking for a way to dispatch Mary without arousing suspicion. He'll want to shoot her whenever he can conveniently blame it on someone else. For example, he might shoot her if she's running along the wall and blame it on Lord Tristan's men or shoot her while the Cybermen are spiriting her away through the tunnel ('accidentally' hitting her when the Cybermen were the true targets).

CHANGING HISTORY

Historically, Mary's death is still 12 years away so killing her now changes history. If she still has any, Mary Stuart (or her attendant Mary) will spend their Story Points to avoid being injured. If she is out of Story Points, or you deem it more appropriately dramatic, she could be mortally wounded 12 years early.

Assuming that the characters can get to her in time, a 'mortal wound' in the Elizabethan era is not necessarily a mortal wound for a modern or futuristic character to operate on.

Imagine the surprise from Gabriel or Lord Percival when the characters save Mary from a bullet wound that would normally be fatal or imagine the players having to stop Lord Percival from doing something to "ease the pain" when her wound is treatable!

Alternatively, Mary's death 12 years early could be mitigated. Perhaps Elizabeth allows the fiction that her cousin is alive to continue for 12 more years while Walsingham ferrets out spies. Since Mary's handwriting was particularly easy for forgers to copy, the Queen could get someone else (Mary Seton, perhaps) to impersonate her.

Since Mary spent her last 12 years imprisoned, you could fix history at the invasion of the Spanish Armada. Prior to that, perhaps the Catholic sympathisers rally behind a new claimant to the English throne (or perhaps get James VI of Scotland to reconsider his mother's faith). Mary I had married a Spanish prince, so Spain certainly has a claim to press before deciding to go to war.

Alternatively, maybe things calm down a bit until the Spaniards decide to launch their invasion.

ENDING THE SIEGE

Neither Lord Tristan nor the Cybermen want to continue the siege long enough for reinforcements to arrive. If the castle hasn't been breached by the time the Cybermats and one or two Cybermen have been destroyed, then Lord Tristan orders a withdrawal. He does this with a heavy heart (relatively speaking), as he knows that he'll probably be besieged himself in a couple of days.

The Cybermen assure Lord Tristan that this is only a temporary setback, as a siege takes time and by then more Cybermen will be ready to engage the enemy. The Cybermen suggest converting the Earl's own people, something he'd initially hoped to avoid. It is this promise that keeps Lord Tristan's spirits up as he orders the retreat.

MARY'S ESCAPE

It's possible that the Cybermen may succeed in rescuing Mary Stuart. In this case, the Marys are taken to Hawkwood castle while Lord Tristan summons reinforcements. The Cybermen will split their forces between their ship and the castle to protect her. The characters can either stage a commando-style raid or organise a siege of their own to recapture Mary. They'll receive aid from Anne Steele (see the **Unexpected Help** sidebar) if they attempt such a plan.

⚙ 4. TAKING THE FIGHT TO THE ENEMY

The characters are going to want to find and destroy the Cybermen base at some point. Their crashed ship lies only a few miles from Lord Tristan's castle in Hawksfordshire. Getting to the ship is fraught with danger, as Cybermats and Lord Tristan's patrols swarm southern Hawkwood.

Once the Cybermen threat is ended, the characters have completed the adventure and can safely head off for new adventures. It's possible that a loose end, such as Lord Tristan or a Cybermat, may remain at large, setting the stage for a potential sequel.

UNEXPECTED HELP

While a devout Catholic, Anne Steele, Tristan's younger sister, has no desire to be in league with the Devil in order to make England Catholic again. In spite of Tristan's best efforts to keep her away from them, Anne has seen the Cybermen and believes them to be demons. She's certain that they have spread their unholy poison to him as well. So far, she's managed to hide this from her brother and he desires to keep her at his side as a valuable marital prospect to win a powerful noble to his cause.

Gamemasters can use Anne to push the plot along as convenient. She might sneak out of Hawksford Castle one night and arrive at Mortenbury, wishing to speak with Lord Percival. She could offer any information that she'd rationally know, such as the whereabouts of the Cybermen's ship and their refusal to move their 'lair' to a more defensible location. She can also tell them that Hawkwood is better patrolled in the south than the north.

ANNE STEELE

AWARENESS	3	PRESENCE	3
COORDINATION	2	RESOLVE	3
INGENUITY	3	STRENGTH	1

SKILLS
Athletics 2, Convince 1, Craft 2, Knowledge 2, Marksman 0, Medicine 1, Subterfuge 2, Survival 1.

TECH LEVEL: 4   **STORY POINTS:** 3

HAWKWOOD

How to approach Hawkwood poses an interesting problem. Entering the woods from the south makes it much easier to follow the Cybermen's tracks but almost certainly gets them noticed. Entering the woods from the north enables the characters to move about unnoticed but its harder to follow the Cybermen.

Should the characters approach from the south then the tracks can be followed with an Awareness + Survival roll (Difficulty 9). Characters approaching from the north should spend a Story Point to 'happen upon' the spacecraft, unless they realise that the Cybermats entered the River Morten from Hawkwood. By following the river the characters have a chance at finding the tracks with an Awareness + Survival roll (Difficulty 18).

Hawkwood is heavily patrolled in the south by knights on horseback and sentinels (use English Soldier statistics, see pg. 44) posted at all major roads. These soldiers are mind controlled by the Cybermen and avoid going near it. A few Cybermats are also positioned close to the ship.

- **Cyber-Detector:** A character with the Boffin trait can do some Jiggery-Pokery to create a gadget that can detect any type of energy readings or metals of a Cyberman alloy. A simple radio wave detector would also work, as the Cybermen are broadcasting their position to their Cyber-fleet.

- **Farmers in Disguise:** The characters can fool the sentinels into believing that they are hypnotised farmers if they ride a cart and have 'victims' (other characters) held captive in the cart.

- **For England!** The characters might wait for reinforcements, in which case they might be able to convince the Earl of Shrewsbury to organise a full-scale incursion into Hawkwood, distracting the Cybermen enough so they can slip into the spaceship.

THE CYBERMEN'S SPACESHIP

The Cybermen's spaceship is an advance scout vessel. It contains no heavy weapons other than the mounted laser cannons that were destroyed in the crash. Nevertheless most of the internal systems remain intact. The spaceship has a crew of two with enough conversion chambers to convert two more at a time (these chambers also serve as repair bays for the Cybermen).

In the week that the Cybermen have been here they've managed to create four more Cybermen.

As the characters approach the clearing in the forest they will note that this clearing seems almost regular. As they get closer they can see the shiny outline of a small flying saucer that has obviously crashed here, judging by the dents and scorch marks on the underside of the craft and the downed trees that have only recently been cleared.

There seems to be only one entrance which has been dug out through the soil. Above, an open hatch sports a large antenna dish that is pointed toward the heavens.

The spaceship is a Spartan affair, as the Cybermen don't need living quarters. The ship has three levels. The smallest of these is the piloting section at the top of the ship with space for up to three (or four, snugly) Cybermen, although it only has seats for two. There is also a laser cannon, but the Cybermen have been unwilling to reroute the necessary power to make it functional again (they feel that their personal weapons and the Cybermats are enough to deal with any problems from the locals).

The second level is the conversion chamber, where the Cybermen make more of their own kind. The conversion process is fully automated but takes several hours to complete.

The third, lowest level is the storage area and engines. This was the most heavily damaged part of the ship in the crash and although the engine can still generate power the ship's ability to fly is permanently crippled. Most of the Cybermen spare parts were also damaged. Thus far the Cybermen have been able to piece together enough parts for ten more Cybermen.

The engine's ability to generate power relies on a solar power source. The Cybermen used their emergency solar satellite to provide this. The antenna protruding from the top of the ship is collecting the solar energy reflected down by the satellite in concentrated form.

There is a security camera and lock on the main hatch into the spaceship (it opens into the second level). Bypassing the lock requires an Ingenuity + Technology roll (Difficulty 18). Bypassing the security camera is trickier; unless the characters are pretending to be hypnotised soldiers or camouflaged Cybermen, then they'll have to work fast and hope no one is looking. Spotting the camera before being seen requires an appropriate roll at Difficulty 12.

The doors between levels aren't normally locked, as the Cybermen believe that the locals are too primitive to get inside the hatch.

If the characters manage to sabotage or harm Cybermen inside the ship, a signal will be broadcast to Lord Tristan and any hypnotised soldiers.

The characters could kill all the Cybermen inside the ship, set it to self-destruct, and then have to face Lord Tristan and a half-dozen soldiers.

Here are some more things they might try:

- **Overloading the Ion Drive:** A character can overload the ion drive and cause it to explode by increasing the amount of solar power that is being sent to the generators. This requires an Ingenuity + Technology roll (Difficulty 15), but assumes the character is familiar with Technology Level 6 or higher.

  Once overloaded, the ion drive will roast everything inside the ship within seconds and then cause a small explosion. The explosion consumes the ship and burns out the trees in a 50 metre radius, but otherwise causes no lingering damage to the area.

- **Sabotaging the Antenna:** A makeshift magnifying glass could sabotage the antenna and cause a power surge, disrupting and disabling the Cybermen's ship and initiating a self-destruct fail-safe. This requires the Boffin trait and an Ingenuity + Technology roll (Difficulty 18) to build an Awareness + Technology roll (Difficulty 9) to properly position.

HAWKSFORD CASTLE

Lord Tristan's residence sits on a bluff overlooking the East Bevern River and overlooks the town of Hawksford. A moat surrounds the castle; Lord Tristan also has a nasty surprise there too, as bits of old spears, pikes and blades line the bottom of the moat, hidden beneath the water. Two gatehouses, one to the south and one to the east, control the drawbridges across the moat.

Unlike Mortenbury Castle, Hawksford Castle boasts only a single, larger courtyard, bounded on three sides by walls and to the west by the three-story residence. Six high towers are positioned along the wall. The south-westernmost of these, Guy's Tower, is connected to the residence and contains the dungeon. Inside the courtyard, Tristan's forces and support staff are encamped. He keeps a personal guard of 60 soldiers; 200 more in the courtyard are a mixture of mercenaries and soldiers loaned from sympathetic lords. Each tower contains a cannon, and there are four more sitting on top of the main residence. Unlike Mortenbury, Hawksford Castle doesn't have cannons at water level.

LORD TRISTAN'S LAIR

The characters could find themselves going to Hawksford Castle for a variety of reasons. They may wish to learn more about Lord Tristan, "free" Mary Stuart, or be brought there in irons. In most cases, Lord Tristan is coolly confident, especially given that he is mostly a Cyberman.

This is an excellent time for the characters to discover that Anne Steele is not comfortable with her brother's actions. Indeed, she doesn't even know that he's been converted (although she suspects he's been bewitched in some way) and immediately turns against him if the truth is revealed. If approached, Anne offers any assistance she can, including the location of the bolt hole beneath the main residence building that leads beneath the river to emerge in Hawkwood on the other side (see **Unexpected Help**, on pg. 48).

Because of his partial conversion, Lord Tristan poses a lingering problem for the players. Even if the Cybermen are destroyed, Lord Tristan's body can live on for centuries. Unfortunately for him, his head still ages normally and as time goes on he'll have to disguise his increasingly grotesque appearance. Without further treatment, Lord Tristan's head will die within the next century or two, leaving a headless Cyberman wandering aimlessly about.

- **Escape from the Dungeon:** Characters left in the dungeon can use Coordination + Subterfuge (Difficulty 12) to pick the lock and escape,

providing that they have a means to do so. A guard is stationed here at all times, but it's a boring post and he is often asleep or easily duped into getting too close.

- **Mary's Aid:** While it's good to have Anne Steele on their side, the characters may want to bring Mary Stuart around to their cause. While Mary relishes the chance at freedom and a throne, the characters may point out that Lord Tristan doesn't stand a chance of succeeding even with his metal friends. When he does fail, it is in Mary's best interests not to be perceived as having been in collusion with him. Once she is convinced, Mary will do what is asked of her to help the characters.

✿ AFTERMATH

Assuming that the characters succeed, the Earl of Shrewsbury arrives and immediately throws a feast in their honour. The Earl tells them that they must come with him to London to get a proper reward from the Queen, and Dr Field (if still alive and still an ally) hints that Walsingham — possibly Queen Elizabeth herself — wants a word with them.

In short, it's the perfect opportunity for the characters to slip away with the knowledge that history is secure — a smart move if they've previously had a run in with the Queen...

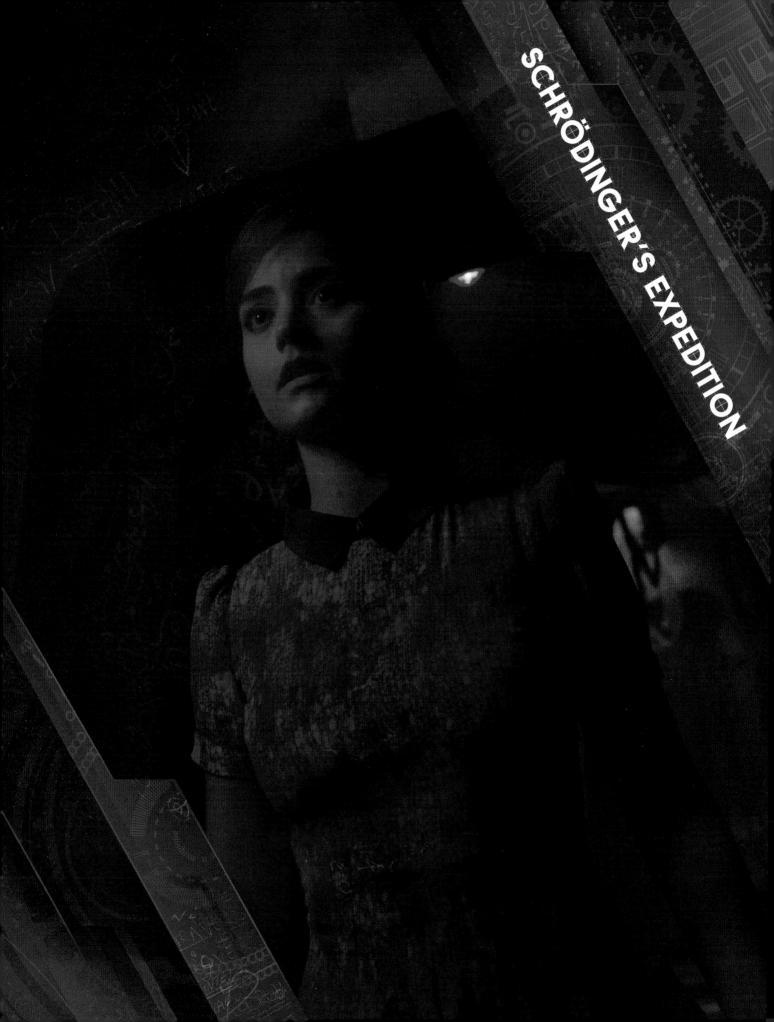

SCHRÖDINGER'S EXPEDITION

Once upon a time, before the Time War, there was a Time Lord and a time capsule – like the Doctor's TARDIS but a different model. Telepathically bonded together like all time capsules and their pilots, the pair travelled through time and space, much like the Doctor and his TARDIS. Until there was an accident, and the Time Lord died. Stricken and alone with that telepathic contact lost, the time capsule did the only thing it felt it could do; it took itself far far away from all civilisation, intent on self-destruction. However, the overload of the time capsule's drive systems did not go according to plan. Rather than unleashing enough energy to vaporise itself, the breach in space and time turned the time capsule inside out – all that remained was a maze of corridors and rooms loosely joined together in a seemingly random order around a rift in the fabric of space-time – the final death scream of a time capsule. That silent scream has continued until now.

⚙ ADVENTURE SYNOPSIS

However they arrive, the characters arrive inside a corridor. There are no indications to what they've materialised aboard, there are no signs or insignia. If they have reasonable sensors or some sort of portable scanner, they may be able to tell that they've arrived on some sort of large space station in deep space. However, this space station is constructed in a very haphazard kind of way. There doesn't seem to be

any real organisation to it, and there are no obvious docking areas. Sensors should also indicate that there's a hugely powerful time/space breach in the centre of the construction, and that the characters are not alone – there are other humanoid life signs on board, grouped together, not far from wherever the characters arrived. Not far from those is the power signature of some sort of long-range vessel. Lastly, there are some odd life-sign readings around the area – slow moving and sluggish things that seem to be gathering together around the location of the first set of life-signs.

This place was once a time capsule, but it has been distorted by its own suicide attempt. Now all the rooms that were inside are on the outside, and the transcendental geometry that made it look smaller on the outside than the inside is itself inside, ripping a hole in the fabric of space and time. The result is that pockets of the whole place are moving through parallel dimensions – a fact that the characters will soon discover...

⚙ ANOMALY IV

For a thousand years the dead time capsule has floated in space, visible in the night sky from the planet Pilatedes. The Quorum – a human civilisation that inhabits Pilatedes – once worshipped the object as a god, but these are enlightened times for them and now they have mounted an expedition to it. The Quorum has named this floating complex of rooms and corridors "Anomaly IV", or more simply "The Anomaly."

The Anomaly is very large by spaceship standards. One could spend months exploring its reaches, from the outer rooms that contain bedrooms, dormitories, small nooks and crannies for storage, a wardrobe room, a canteen and even a swimming pool, to the inner locations where things get stranger with warehouses and environmental recreations for different atmospheres. It has basic life support – heat and light are provided by the systems embedded in each corridor and each room. There is breathable air too. On the other hand, any systems that are connected to the "brain" of the Anomaly are broken and cannot be fixed.

Over thousands of years, the Anomaly has been 'colonised' by a number of space-faring species. To date, none of these have been intelligent, probably due to the distances involved in reaching the place. Rather, the species that live on the Anomaly now are those whose life-cycles involve travelling long distances through space and surviving for long periods without food. These have built up a kind of eco-system within the vessel; one that both the explorers and the characters will have to contend with.

CORRIDORS

The corridors in Anomaly IV are oblong in cross-section – definitely designed by and intended to carry humanoids of about the same size as humans. Light is diffuse and seems to come from above. While both the ceiling and floor are a dull grey colour, the walls are white and display a tiled pattern on them, composed of large octagons separated by smaller squares. Some of the octagons have access panels beneath them that can be removed from the walls in order to look at the circuitry behind (though the majority of this is broken as described above).

No corridor ever extends past around 60 feet without coming across a junction of some kind, and the insides of the Anomaly could well begin to resemble some sort of complex maze if the characters don't employ any kind of technique for determining where they are, or where they've been.

In addition, some areas of the Anomaly are darker than others, where the lighting has simply failed or has been damaged (see **Wolves**, pg. 57) In these areas the darkness is total and a torch of some kind will be required. Encounters with any of the denizens of Anomaly IV in these dark areas are likely to have an additional edge to them.

WAREHOUSES

The characters may discover one or more warehouses during their exploration of Anomaly IV. In a normal working time capsule there are a number of outlying warehouses and storage spaces that can be used to keep supplies or passengers. Here in the Anomaly the warehouses are empty, their contents mostly eaten by the Silverfish or converted by Milk

Mushrooms into compost. If you fancy messing with your players' heads, this is a good place to dump random clues and ideas to other places and times: the sorts of flotsam and jetsam that a time capsule might have picked up on its travels; perhaps a jumpsuit with the logo of the Sirius Conglomerate, a space suit or a sonic blaster. The warehouses are an ideal place for an enterprising Gamemaster to leave red herrings suggesting that Anomaly IV has some deeper meaning to it. In its travels before becoming the Anomaly this time capsule might have picked up various bits of technology from the races that are common in the universe. A Dalek weapon arm or a Judoon helmet would put the characters off the scent of what's really going on.

If your characters are less than experienced space and time travellers feel free to have them be accompanied by the Scientific Expedition when they explore a warehouse.

LIFE FORMS INHABITING THE ANOMALY

Milk Mushrooms

Any space traveller who has travelled for a period of time is aware of Milk Mushrooms. These unassuming flat yellow fungi – usually around 12 inches in diameter – are one of the most widespread life forms known in the galaxy. The mushrooms exude a thick, milky liquid that is almost universally safe to consume, but which is loaded with the microscopic spores of the mushrooms. These spores are taken with whatever creature consumes the milk and are incredibly hardy, able to survive for years even in a vacuum by entering a state of cryptobiosis. Once a spore settles on a surface containing organic matter it latches on and grows, converting the surface material into biomass.

Regardless of whether the Milk Mushrooms aboard Anomaly IV were brought on board by its original inhabitants or one of the species that has come on

WHAT MIGHT ONE FIND IN A TARDIS WAREHOUSE?

The following is a list of possible artefacts that could be found in a TARDIS warehouse, not all of which are entirely useful, but could be adventure hooks all of their own...

A Musical Instrument: This is a small spherical object, appearing to be cast out of solid bronze with glyphs and markings on it in High Gallifreyan. When picked up it reacts to the mental state of the bearer, emitting music that matches their emotional state.

A Medical Scanner: The medical scanner is a wet-feeling gel, looking like blue silly putty. When laid over a living being (and living being is quite a broad definition for the gel) it projects holographic information about them, but in alien script. With some experimentation and experience it can be used to give a +1 to rolls involving the Medicine skill.

An Alchemist/Apothecary's Kit: This is a leather case, stiffened with wood on the inside, that holds an array of small glass bottles. The bottles contain a variety of chemicals that might be used by a witch doctor or hedge alchemist such as sodium, saltpetre, gold flakes and mercury. It should be noted that many of these chemicals are poisonous if ingested. The kit could be sold as an antique any time after Earth's 20th century.

A Map: In an ornate gunmetal grey scroll-case, covered with odd symbols is an old, faded and grey map – like a treasure map but covered with pictures of stars and planets. Enough detail is provided to allow a trained individual to recognise individual star systems, and the map might be used to navigate by. Of course, one of the planets has more detail than the rest and there are planetary co-ordinates marked with a large red "X."

A Venus Mantrap: A potted plant, kept in a glass-domed container, the glass long faded and cloudy with age. The plant looks very similar to a Venus flytrap, but prefers mammals for food rather than insects. This one is a baby but is still capable of attacking and causing 0/1/2 damage. Close examination indicates that the plant is actually a cyborg with tiny wires forming circuits within its leaves.

board since, they have colonised as much space as possible. Some corridors are entirely painted yellow with the mushrooms, though in other areas they have been pruned back by the other life forms in the Anomaly, notably the Silverfish.

Silverfish

An insectoid creature that lives off of the Milk Mushrooms in the endless corridors and chambers of Anomaly IV, the Silverfish might prove uncomfortable for the characters to deal with. About the size of a small dog and possessed of segmented bodies with a metallic sheen, Silverfish have tiny compound eyes hidden under the chitinous plates that make up their 'faces' and large gripping mandibles. Their many legs are short and almost hidden under their bodies, giving them the appearance almost of snakes.

Silverfish probably look more frightening than they are, more or less uninterested in anything other than the Milk Mushrooms that grow in abundance inside the Anomaly. In fact, they prefer solitude and generally flee if they encounter another race. A Silverfish moves at roughly the speed of a sprinting human; they are extremely hard to catch, moving with a sinuous curving motion like a snake.

SILVERFISH

AWARENESS	3	PRESENCE	1
COORDINATION	4	RESOLVE	2
INGENUITY	1	STRENGTH	2

SKILLS
Subterfuge 3, Survival 3.

TRAITS
Alien
Cowardly
Environmental (Space)
Keen Senses
Quick Reflexes
Size – Tiny (Major)

STORY POINTS: 1-2

Silverfish live as parasites for the most part, inside the junk piles and refuse collection points of large settlements. The community in Anomaly IV live in equilibrium with the Milk Mushrooms, both species limiting each others' numbers for the most part, though the Silverfish are also hunted by the Wolves. Silverfish require very little by way of food in

order to power themselves, their simple bodies being a miracle of billions of years of refinement by evolution. If one is ejected from a spaceship travelling at some faster-than-light speed it might be found following the same course, still alive, a hundred years later, ready to latch onto the first thing it comes across, be that a spaceship, a planet or an asteroid. There exist asteroids in space that are riddled with dormant Silverfish waiting for something to pass by so that they can colonise it and begin their life-cycle anew.

Characters might encounter a Silverfish hive, full of wriggling bodies, pallid eggs the size of a human head and piles of festering Milk Mushroom material. In these environments the Silverfish are protecting their home and young, and are much more likely to be aggressive to any invader.

Wolves

The Wolves are a predatory race that arrived in the Anomaly with some humanoids, decades ago. Whether they were pets or hunting animals is unknown. What's for sure is that there is no longer any sign of the humanoids that brought them. The Wolves are now a power in their own right within the tiny ecosystem of the Anomaly.

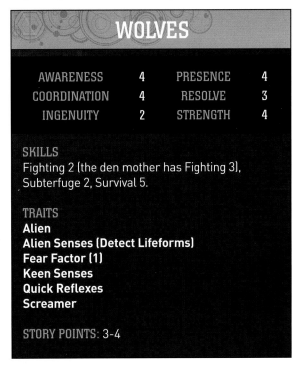

WOLVES

AWARENESS	4	PRESENCE	4
COORDINATION	4	RESOLVE	3
INGENUITY	2	STRENGTH	4

SKILLS
Fighting 2 (the den mother has Fighting 3),
Subterfuge 2, Survival 5.

TRAITS
Alien
Alien Senses (Detect Lifeforms)
Fear Factor (1)
Keen Senses
Quick Reflexes
Screamer

STORY POINTS: 3-4

Wolves are black in colour, and as such tend to keep to the shadows where their natural camouflage prevents them from being easily detected. Their bodies are furred and long, more like an Earth stoat or ferret than an actual wolf. They share a couple of characteristics with their namesakes, though – the first is that they are entirely carnivorous. Secondly, they emit a howl when they are hunting, both to terrify their prey and to communicate position with each other. Unlike Earth wolves they are quite intelligent – enough to know how to do things like increasing the chances of a successful hunt by chewing through electrical cables and causing a power blackout in a particular area of the Anomaly.

Perhaps because of this intelligence, the Wolves aboard the Anomaly have learned to use the two dimensions to their advantage and have gained the ability to swap between universes whenever and wherever they like, hunting their prey in one universe and then attacking in the other, appearing to spring en masse from nowhere with a deafening howl. From the party's point of view the Wolves may be able to follow them from one universe to another during an attack.

Where they fall down is in tactics. Though they know how to do the "attack under darkness and in small numbers" tactic that works for them in the wild, they don't understand the idea of luring an enemy into a trap. But if they don't have the advantage of darkness they can be cut to pieces by the weapons carried by the Military Expedition.

The Wolves are slowly decreasing in number, primarily because they have no variety in their food source. They currently amount to less than a hundred individuals. They sleep in a pack like their namesakes, and have chosen the warmest location on the Anomaly: at the centre of the structure with the Dimensional Disturbance. It's there that the wolves' leader dwells as well – the den mother. The mother is similar to the other wolves but a little bigger and better fed.

THE DIMENSIONAL DISTURBANCE

A TARDIS contains a powerful energy source at its core, strong enough to open a path into the Vortex: typically a black hole known as the Eye of Harmony. It was this energy source that the time capsule overloaded when it tried to commit suicide. Unfortunately, both the Vortex and transcendental mathematics are tricky things, and the resulting explosion mangled space and time, with the final result that the capsule became the Anomaly with all of its internal structure on the outside.

But that wasn't the end of it: time and space are still warped within the vicinity of Anomaly IV, to the extent that the characters will end up literally stepping between parallel universes. What's worse,

TIME LORDS AND THE ANOMALY

Surely a Time Lord would recognise a TARDIS, right? Well, not necessarily. Arriving in a time capsule for the first time, the semi-telepathic Time Lord can 'feel' the machine around them. It quite literally speaks to them. In an environment like the Anomaly, where the brain of the machine is long dead, they will feel nothing.

To the passing Time Lord, the Anomaly is just like any other space station or vessel with a lot of cramped and short corridors – and there certainly seem to be a lot of those in space! A particularly clever Time Lord might recognise the order and pattern of the rooms in the Anomaly as the sort of thing a time capsule might generate, but this is highly unlikely (a character with the Time Traveller, Time Lord, Time Traveller, Feel the Turn of the Universe or Vortex traits might pick up on this with an Awareness + Science skill check, Difficulty 20.)

Any seasoned space and time traveller will notice that the Anomaly isn't built quite like most space stations. There are no sealable bulkheads. There are no obvious docking points. Everything seems to be laid out in a haphazard fashion rather than in a properly organised manner.

SCHRÖDINGER'S EXPEDITION

this has been exacerbated by the close proximity of expeditions from two different universes at the same time. Slowly but surely the two universes are coming to occupy the same space, and that can't be good.

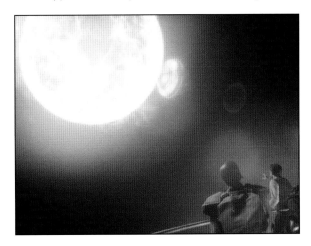

In one universe, Anomaly IV is being investigated by an expedition from the Quorum College; an institution of learning on the planet Pilatedes where learning is prized over all else. This expedition is tasked with discovering what the Anomaly is, who built it and why, and what knowledge can be gleaned from it.

In the other universe, the Anomaly is also under investigation from an expedition from Pilatedes. However, these humanoids are representatives of the Quorum Conflict; a war machine intent on conquering everything it comes across. These soldiers are investigating the Anomaly with a view to finding if it can be used as a weapon.

When flipped between the parallel universes, the characters should notice nothing at all; no jarring effects, neither light nor sound. The Anomaly in both universes is the same; it is the eye of the temporal storm, after all.

The characters should not be able to predict or control the journey between universes either until later in the adventure when both expeditions become aware of them and develop the means to predict where rifts between dimensions will open. This provides a powerful tool for the Gamemaster, and one that should be used sparingly so that the players don't feel like they're being railroaded through the adventure.

You can use dimensional rifts to spring undetectable encounters on your players (who might be walking down a corridor and suddenly find there's an armed team of soldiers behind them) or allow them to get out of a locked room.

THE QUORUM

In the two universes, the Quorum have had quite a different history, diverging when the Anomaly was created. The object became visible in the sky with the naked eye from Pilatedes a thousand years ago, during a period of social upheaval and discovery for the Pilatedeans – similar to the Renaissance period on Earth. Every witch doctor and semi-religious leader incorporated the Anomaly into their belief systems, but a single astronomer by the name of Professor Goran used science to prove that the object was just another body in space like Pilatedes itself. The discovery sparked controversy and conflict, which rapidly spread across Pilatedes' major civilisations.

In one universe, the conflict lasted only a decade until the cooler heads of the scientific community prevailed, bringing an end to the war and establishing the Quorum College as a place of learning so that superstition could never be the cause of bloodshed again. In the other universe, differing opinions on which religion 'owned' the Anomaly have kept a cold war going for a thousand years. Both sides of the war maintain weapons and armies, and there is a constant threat of violence breaking out.

⚙ THE SCIENTIFIC EXPEDITION – QUORUM COLLEGE

The Quorum College is Pilatedes' biggest institute of higher education, built originally as a centre of learning that would prevent superstition from flourishing on the planet. As the College grew and grew it became very much like a town itself, with support staff living there full-time, and students coming in to live and study.

Professors and teachers came to live there too, and in the present day the College is the dominant place of employment and the city has come to be known after the College itself.

The Scientific Expedition consists of 20 scientists and doctors from the College as well as a starship crew of five. The starship crew either remain with their ship or act as guard for the place where they tethered and cut their way into the Anomaly, so it's likely the scientists will meet the characters first. While all of the expedition crew are armed (with small laser weaponry) they are unlikely to adopt a tactic of "fire first and ask questions later." Rather they will try to investigate before acting even in self-defence.

It's important to note that the members of the Quorum College expedition are strangers to war. Their homeworld has never experienced a world war and if the topic comes up in conversation they will describe it as a peaceful utopia.

PROFESSOR KELLY-HOTEL

Professor Kelly-Hotel (nobody knows if he actually has a first name!) is the leader of the Quorum College expedition. He is a force of curiosity, constantly looking for the next thing that he can pick up, examine, dissect and learn everything about. When he is examining something his attention is laser-sharp, like there

is nothing else in the universe but the object of his fascination. The characters can expect to come under the microscope of Kelly-Hotel's attention when they first meet the Scientific Expedition.

PROFESSOR KELLY-HOTEL

AWARENESS	4	PRESENCE	3
COORDINATION	2	RESOLVE	4
INGENUITY	5	STRENGTH	2

SKILLS
Knowledge 3, Medicine 1, Science 4, Technology 3.

TRAITS
Arrogant: He knows just how clever he is.
Boffin: One of Pilatedes' foremost minds.
Insatiable Curiosity
Technically Adept: He is the smartest guy in the room.

TECH LEVEL: 5   STORY POINTS: 6

However, more often than not the objects that Kelly-Hotel scrutinises will turn out to be relatively mundane, which the Professor thinks is below him. When this occurs he will discard the objects of his fascination, forgetting them and focusing on something new. This is likely to be the case with the characters; once he has met and talked to them, the Professor will lose interest, forget that they exist and move on to examine something different and new. This could cause problems for getting things done later down the line!

The Professor is a tall, thin, dynamic man in his late thirties, quite young to hold the position that he does. He has black hair, pulled back from his temples with a small ponytail at the back. He moves with nervous energy, frequently changing what he's looking at and moving his body back and forth as he talks.

DOCTOR JULIET SMITH-PAPA

Juliet Smith-Papa is the medical doctor of the Quorum College expedition. While she is central to the expedition's success in terms of curing the ill, her day-to-day research duties are a little light, especially in the relatively simple biological habitat of the Anomaly. Therefore, she may be assigned as a liaison of sorts to the characters rather than take up Professor Kelly-Hotel's time.

DOCTOR SMITH-PAPA

AWARENESS	4	PRESENCE	3
COORDINATION	2	RESOLVE	3
INGENUITY	4	STRENGTH	2

SKILLS
Craft 1, Knowledge 2, Medicine 2, Science 4, Technology 3.

TRAITS
Boffin
Insatiable Curiosity: Smith-Papa is intrigued by everything – and everyone – around her.
Resourceful Pockets: The pockets of her utility vest could hide almost anything.
Technically Adept

TECH LEVEL: 5   STORY POINTS: 4

The characters should also get the once-over from Smith-Papa to determine whether or not they have any dangerous pathogens on them, and whether their particular sub-genome has been seen before

(it should be noted that the Quorum College will not know about any races other than human; they will be enormously excited to scan anyone 'exotic').

Smith-Papa is a true scientist; curious to a fault and open-minded about the odd and strange. The assignment to Anomaly IV is a dream for her; a chance to investigate something that nobody understands at all. She secretly believes that the creator of the Anomaly dwells in the centre of the structure, and that cosmic secrets will be revealed to those that make it there.

In terms of appearance, Smith-Papa wears the blue overalls of the whole expedition, and has a utility vest with various scientific instruments placed within it. The vest should be treated as a running joke - she can pull almost anything out of that vest. She is in her mid-forties, hair greying around the temples and beginning to thin out a little.

VIOLET SIERRA-GAMMA

Violet's a young graduate student specialising in block transfer computational physics. Visiting the Anomaly is the culmination of a lifelong dream for her, and she fought hard to get this assignment. She believes that the Anomaly is the most important discovery in the history of the College, possibly in the history of the Quorum people and that it must be protected at all costs. It's the key to the future.

She has short but unruly black hair and wears an eclectic mix of badges and subculture symbols on her jumpsuit. She's never without her pocket computer.

Coincidentally, there's another version of Violet in the Military Expedition.

VIOLET SIERRA-GAMMA

AWARENESS	3	PRESENCE	2
COORDINATION	3	RESOLVE	4
INGENUITY	4	STRENGTH	2

SKILLS
Convince 2, Knowledge 1, Science 4, Technology 3.

TRAITS
Insatiable Curiosity

TECH LEVEL: 5   STORY POINTS: 4

PLAYING THE SCIENTIFIC EXPEDITION

The Scientific Expedition are well-prepared, well-meaning, utterly lovely people. They come from a world that's close to being a blissful utopia. All this means that they're worryingly over-confident, a bit egotistical and much too convinced of their own genius and ability to deal with the universe. They believe that they can unravel the secrets of the Anomaly. Suggestions that meddling with the Anomaly is unwise, or that the Anomaly is the product of a science vastly superior to their own, will be ignored by these brave men and women of science!

⊛ THE MILITARY EXPEDITION – QUORUM CONFLICT

The Military Expedition also comes from Pilatedes, but their planet is not the same one as the scientists'. Religious and philosophical differences have perpetuated a cold war on Pilatedes for close to a thousand years. The Quorum Conflict is an elite fighting force from the largest nation on Pilatedes. Eager for some sign that the Anomaly fits within their own cosmology and in the belief that they will find some holy weapon aboard, they have organised this voyage. That said, even on this version of Pilatedes time marches on and superstition is beginning to make way for a more scientific and less faith-based way of thinking.

The Military Expedition is small, the better to keep the cost of transit low. A platoon of 25 soldiers are supported by drone guns that are deployed where their ship has docked.

These are career military men and they know nothing else. The characters will likely be seen as "civilians" and should be treated with little respect until they prove their worth to the platoon. Indeed, "civilian" should always be said with a little bit of a sneer, like it's a dirty word.

It should also be noted that the Military Expedition are superstitious and deeply faithful – not quite zealots, but likely to utter a prayer before going into conflict or to clutch at a religious symbol worn around the neck in times of stress.

COMMANDER YARDLEY-BRAVO

The woman who controls the Military Expedition would much rather be at home. She is military, and the military fight in the military. They do not waste time and resources on travelling to strange space stations on a fool's errand for a weapon that may or may not even exist. She's had just about enough of this expedition and it shows: she's angry and officious, just waiting for some kind of problem to arise so she can unleash her wrath upon it. And the characters would be a fine example of that. While she can't

kill the strangers she finds in the Anomaly – they represent a potential source of information about the place – she's definitely in favour of torturing all of their information out, not caring if they live or die.

Yardley-Bravo is an Amazonian figure just shy of six-feet tall with clearly defined muscles. Her uniform is an immaculate royal blue, her boots and riot helmet shiny black. There's a rumour amongst the rest of the Conflict Expedition that she gets up an hour before everyone else in the billet to make sure that her uniform is just so.

Inactivity over the last couple of months has softened the Commander's features, but only a little. Unlike most of her troops, Yardley-Bravo doesn't wear a religious symbol around her neck. She doesn't object to that behaviour but it doesn't have a place in her command style.

COMMANDER YARDLEY-BRAVO

AWARENESS	3	PRESENCE	3
COORDINATION	4	RESOLVE	4
INGENUITY	3	STRENGTH	4

SKILLS
Athletics 2, Fighting 3, Marksman 3, Survival 3.

TRAITS
Brave: Yardley-Bravo firmly believes in leading from the front.
Quick Reflexes
Tough: She's tall, well built and doesn't have time for your nonsense.
Voice of Authority: Everyone knows she's in charge.

TECH LEVEL: 5   STORY POINTS: 6

LIEUTENANT HALL-KILO

Chosen for his efficacy and efficiency in equal measure, Lieutenant Hall-Kilo is the straight-laced and no-nonsense subordinate to Commander Yardley-Bravo. He knows his superior is bored and unimpressed with the orders the group have been given, but there is a spark of wonder deep down inside him.

This is a mission to something wondrous and amazing in the middle of a war and he appreciates the contrast. That isn't to say that he's not a military

man; just that he can see the bigger picture of what Anomaly IV is and what it could mean for the Quorum Conflict.

This translates as some sympathy for the plight of the characters. Not enough to make the Lieutenant disobey the spirit of his orders, but he won't treat the characters badly; perhaps not clapping them in irons in a prison cell when the cell itself will do the job, or perhaps advising Yardley-Bravo against the idea of torturing their prisoners.

Hall-Kilo is a little short to be a soldier, his body and muscles wiry rather than bulky; if he were a commanding officer he might have trouble from his men over his height. He is, however, a superb tactician and an excellent subordinate to the more experienced and older Yardley-Bravo.

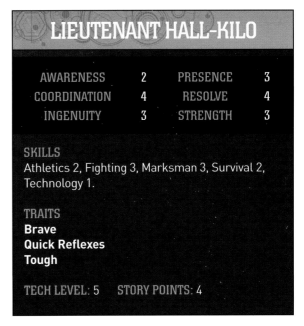

LIEUTENANT HALL-KILO

AWARENESS	2	PRESENCE	3
COORDINATION	4	RESOLVE	4
INGENUITY	3	STRENGTH	3

SKILLS
Athletics 2, Fighting 3, Marksman 3, Survival 2, Technology 1.

TRAITS
Brave
Quick Reflexes
Tough

TECH LEVEL: 5   STORY POINTS: 4

PRIVATE VIOLET SIERRA-GAMMA

Violet's newly assigned to this unit. For her, it's the fulfilment of a dream. Not only does she get to serve under her idol and inspiration, the great Yardley-Bravo, she also gets to go to the Holy Messenger, the divine light that inspired a thousand years of faith and sacrifice. She believes that the Anomaly is a test for the faithful, and that the 'weapon' that Yardley-Bravo searches for is actually a divine power. If Yardley-Bravo embraces religion, she will lead the Quorum Conflict to glorious victory over their enemies.

Unlike her alternate-universe counterpart, this version of Violet keeps her hair closely cropped and her uniform is always crisp and neat. She's never without her sidearm.

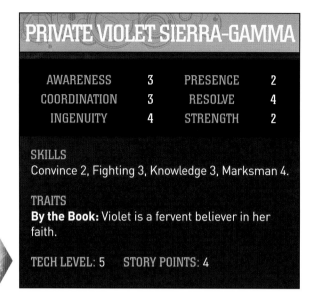

PRIVATE VIOLET SIERRA-GAMMA

AWARENESS	3	PRESENCE	2
COORDINATION	3	RESOLVE	4
INGENUITY	4	STRENGTH	2

SKILLS
Convince 2, Fighting 3, Knowledge 3, Marksman 4.

TRAITS
By the Book: Violet is a fervent believer in her faith.

TECH LEVEL: 5   **STORY POINTS: 4**

PLAYING THE MILITARY EXPEDITION

The Military Expedition aren't necessarily the villains of this scenario, although it is very likely they'll end up taking that role. They come from a world riven by strife and religious wars, so they are paranoid, desperate and quick to use violence and force to achieve their goals. However, they are possibly better prepared for the dangers of the Anomaly. The characters will almost certainly have to use the Military Expedition's weapons to get to the core of the time capsule – the only question is, do they trick, steal or talk their way into getting those weapons?

⚙ 1. ARRIVAL

The characters should arrive at some random point within Anomaly IV – whether they intended to travel here or whether their TARDIS brought them here for reasons of its own is besides the point. Once they are here, they will find that they are unable to leave. They should be able to tell nothing other than the fact that they have arrived in a corridor. There are life-signs nearby (the Scientific Expedition, in this case) and they have arrived in some large space station or similar construct with a large and powerful energy source at its centre. It is likely this energy source that is keeping them from leaving.

The characters will likely want to explore their new surroundings a little, and this should bring them into immediate contact with the expedition of scientists from Pilatedes. The Scientific Expedition are looking for the characters and have sensors and other equipment set up. It's only a matter of time before they're surrounded by nervous looking people in blue uniforms and marched to the expedition's temporary headquarters.

The expedition from Quorum College has made a temporary base in one of the warehouses – a large area filled with Milk Mushrooms and partially broken-down rubbish. The scene is a hive of activity, with almost all of the scientists working away or busy unpacking equipment that they've presumably

lugged from their starship. There are microscopes, computers and even a single isolation tent where close examination will reveal that a Silverfish is being vivisected.

The arrival of the party should cause concern, but not a huge amount – after all, the Quorum College group are using sensors to detect life forms and will be aware that there's more on the Anomaly than themselves. On the other hand they may be surprised to find actual proper humans like themselves, but who are not from their world. The party will be quizzed as to who they are, where they are from, how they got to the Anomaly and what their intentions are. At the same time, the Scientific Expedition will be pleased to explain their own understanding of Anomaly IV – and what they hope to get from their expedition. The party should be introduced to Professor Kelly-Hotel and Doctor Smith-Papa at this point. Here are the answers to a few questions the players might ask:

Where are we?

"This is the Anomaly – a strange object that appeared in the skies of our home world a thousand years ago. We are here to investigate it and find out what we can about who built it and why."

Who are you?

"We are a team of scientists from the Quorum College on the planet of Pilatedes."

How did you get here?

"Our spaceship took three months to reach the Anomaly from our home. We've attached her to the outer shell of the Anomaly and burned our way in, using our own airlock as a seal to prevent the Anomaly's atmosphere from leaking out."

What have you discovered here so far?

"We know that this place is far from natural. It was built by someone, but the structure of the place makes no sense. Where are the docking ports? The artefacts we have found seem to come from any number of different civilisations. There seems to be an energy source at the centre of the Anomaly as well – we don't know what it is, though."

What about the alien life-forms?

"We have encountered a fungus and some large insectoid creatures – neither seems dangerous, and neither have the ability to build something of this size or complexity. We surmise that there is a third predatory race as well – we've seen some chewed insect carcasses that suggest there's something else here."

Unfortunately for the Scientific Expedition the Wolves are also able to detect other life forms in the Anomaly, and they have been tracking the characters' party for a little while. Unwittingly the players have led the Wolves straight to the Scientific Expedition (though this may not be apparent to anyone. It's a nice idea to keep around in case the players need a reason to be 'guilt tripped' into helping out later on down the line rather than returning home or journeying onward in space and time.)

Not long after the party have talked to the science team, the Wolves attack.

The battle with the Wolves should begin with the lights in the warehouse going out. The science team have lights as part of their portable lab set-up, and a chilling high-pitched howl echoes from out of the shadows. The situation should rapidly descend into chaos as the scientists – who aren't really prepared for a battle – fire their lasers into the darkness and there's the occasional scream, or flash of a sleek, furry body darting through a lit area. The tide of battle should eventually turn toward the better-armed scientists but there is a cost for them – Professor Kelly-Hotel has been captured and there are a number of scientists dead. Once Kelly-Hotel has been abducted (taken by the Wolves to feed their young in the heart of the Anomaly) the scientists will be able to see that he is still alive – all the scientists carry a medical implant which tracks their life-signs – and they resolve to go and try to rescue him. The party are free to do whatever they want, but the Professor and the centre of the Anomaly are in the same direction, along with the Wolves.

Leaving the warehouse encampment, the party can be entirely separate to the scientists, or they can be with but a little behind the main group. It's also entirely possible to progress to the next scene if the player group wants to do its own thing and not have anything to do with the scientists' hunt for their captured leader.

WHAT IF THE CHARACTERS AREN'T THE SOCIAL KIND?

If your group of players would prefer to go exploring on their own rather than immediately talk to the Scientific Expedition, don't despair!

Allow them to go explore as much as you like, using some of the example locations given below (under **Journey to the Heart of the Anomaly**). When you feel they've explored enough, have them meet up with the Military Expedition who won't allow them to walk away so easily (moving the flow of the adventure into **The Other Side**, opposite). Then, run the rest of the adventure as written.

⚙ 2. THE OTHER SIDE

While the party are off doing their own thing, looking through the endless corridors of Anomaly IV, they inadvertently slip through parallel dimensions. This should be barely perceptible – possibly just as a brief feeling of panic or loneliness (characters might feel this with an Awareness + Survival roll against a Difficulty of 20. Characters with the Psychic or Feel the Turn of the Universe trait get a bonus of +2.) And then it's over.

Once this effect has taken place the characters will no longer be able to interact with the Scientific Expedition until they have 'crossed back' again. Instead, the places taken by the Scientific Expedition in the 'first' universe are taken by their counterparts.

Note that it's only the Pilatideans who are represented in both universes. There is only one version of the characters. Because of this, the characters always move between universes together.

In the 'second' universe the Military Expedition have also set up an encampment in one of the warehouse areas in the Anomaly. They have also been attacked by the wolves. However, their better grasp of tactics and greater depth of experience with combat allowed them to prevail and slaughter the predators. None of their people have been captured and they are now sending a party to the centre of the Anomaly in search of the energy source. If there's anything to be found here, they assume, it'll be in the area with the most energy output.

The Military Expedition will be very surprised to find the characters suddenly appear on their life-sign detectors and will make a beeline toward them, especially if the party make the transfer between dimensions and 'appear' directly behind them. It will be quite hard to avoid the Military Expedition in the same way that it was possible to avoid the scientists. It'll likely be a surprise for the characters when they find themselves suddenly facing an armed squad of soldiers where they expecting mild-mannered scientists.

The Military Expedition will primarily be interested in taking these unknown humans prisoner and escorting them back to their own encampment – the same warehouse that the Scientific Exhibition from Quorum College, but in this universe it's decorated quite differently. The scientific instruments are gone and replaced with a number of rugged computers-in-briefcases, obviously more advanced than those used by the College staff (the military are better funded at the very least!). There are autonomous gun sentries flanking the entrance.

The military encampment is well guarded so it will be hard for the characters to examine anything they want to without being flanked by armed guards, regardless of whether or not they have made friends with the soldiers. Therefore, they won't have the opportunity to minutely examine everything that's in the camp. It should be obvious, though, that there are a variety of weapons, both big and small. These range from the side-arms that the soldiers carry and the automated gun turrets through to some larger, dangerous-looking objects that look like ray-guns on steroids in the camp.

The characters will be immediately brought to Commander Yardley-Bravo, who will interrogate them on how they got here, what their mission is, whether they know anything about the hostiles on the Anomaly and where their transport is. The interrogation should not be violent; Yardley-Bravo is just looking for an explanation at this stage. However, unless the characters come up with a very convincing-sounding story she'll lock them in a small nearby warehouse, barricading it from the outside – just until she decides what to do with them.

Of course, this is a good opportunity to have the characters unwittingly hop between dimensions again, but don't let this prevent them from trying

several methods of getting out of the warehouse. If you haven't already had them explore a warehouse, now is a good time to do that. However, once again, the dimension hop should be done while nobody is looking. Suddenly the place where the door was in the warehouse is now a blank wall, and the door is elsewhere, open and unguarded. The characters will be free to leave, while back in the military dimension the soldiers will end up scratching their heads.

The characters are now in Kansas once more.

⚙ 3. A TERRIFYING DISCOVERY

The characters may by now be used to the shifting of dimensions or they may be completely confused and expecting soldiers to come and herd them back into their prison cell. They might go looking for the soldiers or they might head off in a different direction altogether. Whichever route they take, it shouldn't take long for them to come back in contact with the Scientific Expedition, still on the hunt for Professor Kelly-Hotel. The scientists are completely unaware of the dimensional instability within Anomaly IV and while they won't openly pooh-pooh the characters' story they have more pressing concerns.

Whichever way the players go next, they'll encounter one of the expeditions sooner rather than later. This should take place in a location where the two expeditions are close (albeit in different universes) or where individual members of both expeditions are close together. Suddenly, with no warning, the paths of two expedition members in the parallel universes intersect. With a horrific shrieking noise like the sound of some enormous discordant and distorted bell – a TARDIS cloister bell but louder, atonal and wrong-sounding – the two exist visibly in the same place at the same time. This is a hard thing to look at, like the effect of crossing your eyes.

Both individuals seem horrified and silently try to pull away – unable to make a sound – only to find that they stretch like elastic, bonded to each other in some metaphysical way. With growing horror they realise that they cannot, and the bonding has damaged them internally. Gulping like goldfish they fall to the ground, dead.

Ideally don't kill off expedition members too often; this should be a horrific scene that comes as a surprise to the party. However, you want the players to be made aware of the deleterious effects of the co-existence of the two universes, and that it can't be allowed to continue. If the death takes place in front of witnesses they'll be suitably horrified and upset. If they can work out what's gone on, the characters may want to try to prevent future occurrences of two people being in exactly the same space at the same time in different universes.

At this point in the adventure, the action can go in one of several different directions. Firstly, the players may choose to help the scientists rescue the Professor.

Secondly, they may split off from the scientists to search for the soldiers, or to explore on their own.

They may also be trying to get back to whatever conveyance they used to get to the Anomaly in the first place. Whichever route they take they should become aware of the dimensional instabilities, explaining the jumps they've been experiencing and telling them that something is terribly wrong in the Anomaly – something that will have dire consequences if it's not fixed fast.

This inspiration might come from the players – an Ingenuity + Science roll (Difficulty 12) with appropriate bonuses from the Time Traveller, Time Lord, Time Traveller, Time Agent, Feel the Turn of the Universe or Vortex traits. With a basic Success result, the character has managed to determine that something's terribly wrong and it's getting worse, but they've made the situation worse just by poking at it. With a Fantastic result the character discovers the problem and the cause of it – the energy source in the centre of the Anomaly.

RELATIONS WITH THE MILITARY

The characters escape the Military Expedition when they leave their dimension and return to that of the Scientific Expedition. This will understandably make the party a dangerous unknown as far as the soldiers are concerned. As a dangerous unknown they're unlikely to be killed out of hand. However, there may have to be some fences mended before the party and the soldiers can work together. This could be because the military see the party as possessing some form of superhuman ability granted to them by the Anomaly, or because the characters offer to help the military achieve their goal of finding a weapon that can be used against their enemy.

The best route to an alliance is for the characters to explain what's going on to Commander Yardley-Bravo. The Commander will eventually listen to them, though she will be hard to convince. Once the Military Expedition know what's happening they'll be more amenable to working with the characters. However, they will naturally be sceptical of their parallel universe cousins. In particular they won't like the idea that the scientists are without any kind of religion. Yardley-Bravo is more focused on the mission than the spiritual outcome of it, so she's more likely to be able to accept the scientists and their secular viewpoint.

Less diplomatic players may never ally with the Military Expedition, instead manipulating them using the dimensional rifts and their wits. Both approaches are perfectly valid.

SCHRÖDINGER'S EXPEDITION

Alternatively the sensors in a TARDIS or similar time machine may be able to detect the issue once they know what they are looking for. Either the scientists or the soldiers may be able to use their equipment to detect rifts in space too.

Space is cracking around the Anomaly. The characters can move freely through the cracks, into and around the two dimensions that are colliding here. However, neither of the expeditions from Pilatedes are able to use the rifts. Both are trapped in their own dimension. Once this discovery is made, it is clear that the rifts are being generated by whatever power source is at the heart of Anomaly IV. It's also clear that the instability will eventually rip both dimensions apart with catastrophic force. The Anomaly has caused both universes to diverge within a radius of itself and both universes cannot occupy the same space indefinitely.

Someone will have to shut the Anomaly down – the characters. It's not clear how long the Anomaly has left, though the presence of sentient life forms from both versions of the planet Pilatedes is hastening the deleterious effect on both the dimensions. The party should notice that when the two expeditions are closer together, more rifts appear between the two universes, and when they move apart the number of rifts lessens.

USING THE RIFTS

While a Gadget with the Scan trait can be used (or made) to detect rifts with a successful Awareness + Technology roll, characters can also spend a Story Point to have a handy rift materialise nearby if they need a quick exit. The Gamemaster can also have characters get swallowed and split up by the rifts, which open and close with alarming speed – perhaps as a consequence of a bad roll.

✵ 4. JOURNEY TO THE HEART OF THE ANOMALY

Presumably the characters will take an interest in reaching the heart of the Anomaly – even if they're not charitable towards the Pilatedeans' fate, they are likely to be self-motivated by either the fact that they're trapped here too, or the impending explosion of their own universe. Both expeditions should be able to give them a map of what's around them, and depending on whether or not the characters have explained fully what's going on they should also be able to provide details of how to use the rifts in space to get from one dimension to the other.

The rifts themselves are invisible, and opaque both to sight and sound, but their location and how long they will be open for can be predicted. Once given some method of predicting where the rifts will be (both expeditions will offer the characters a suitable gadget for doing this if they have a friendly relationship with them.)

However, the rifts aren't all easy to walk through. Some of them may be small or above ground level. If you're feeling mean, or if the situation is desperate, you might like to force the party to roll Coordination + Athletics (Difficulty 18-20) to make it through the rift and into the other dimension. The characters will be able to take anything through a rift that they could comfortably carry with them. So yes to the automatic gun turrets the Military Expedition owns and no to the isolation tent belonging to the Scientific Expedition; the residual artron energy from the characters is what enables them to travel through the rifts. Carrying a sufficiently large item cancels out the carrier's artron energy with its own.

Feel free to make getting to the centre of the Anomaly as easy or as difficult as you feel is required. The centre of the Anomaly is the console room of the time capsule that created it, and the rooms that the characters encounter should gain more individuality and substance as they get further in toward the middle. These are the rooms in which the time capsule's crew lived and worked, the rooms where they ate and where they performed whatever scientific experiments were needed.

With a ship as big as a TARDIS there's no need to ever tidy up a room that is no longer used when it can just be archived further into the structure of the vessel, so these rooms may have been centuries old even before the accident that caused the Anomaly.

Use as many or as few of these as you need:

A CHILD'S BEDROOM

This room is small and contains what should have become a familiar sight to the characters, trash and Milk Mushrooms. However, sifting through the trash one might find a small doll-like object. A child-sized bed is still recognisable amongst the rest of the trash, and the characters might find a few articles of clothing that might belong to a child of 11 or 12.

Among the discarded and broken toys is a small Homunculus. This two-foot-tall toy is an intelligent robot, designed to be a child's playmate, and looks a bit like a teddy bear. The long millennia of abandonment have driven it insane. If the characters accidentally reactivate it, it stalks them through the rest of the Anomaly, looking for opportunities to kill them.

THE CAFETERIA

The room here is broad and wide with a low ceiling, quite unlike any of the other rooms that the characters will have seen up to this point. It is also quite smelly; disused machinery that can still generate food has become thoroughly infested with Milk Mushrooms and the room is swarming with Silverfish. Nevertheless, if the party stay for long enough to look around, they'll find the remains of tables and chairs under all the detritus and crusted over, partially eaten remains of Silverfish. The chairs are designed with humanoids in mind, the same shape and size as the characters themselves.

The food generator will only generate unappetising and pretty unpleasant protein compound, having lost all the recipes that it once had. It's left up to the players as to whether or not they want to try eating any of the stuff anyway after the state the Milk Mushrooms and Silverfish have left the machine in.

Also lurking in this room is a lone Wolf, here to hunt the Silverfish. It won't tackle the characters, but will phase in and out of reality to snack on the Silverfish, which is a very disconcerting sight to witness.

THE LABORATORY

This room represents what the rest of the Anomaly might look like if it wasn't completely covered in Milk Mushrooms and trash. This small room has been left alone by the other denizens of the Anomaly, and it's relatively easy to tell why: chemicals have eaten through the containers they were once kept in and burned through the shelves and counters they were stored on. The floor is covered in a foul-smelling goop, the combination of chemicals, time and disuse.

In one spot of the lab there is a section of flooring that has been corroded badly by the chemicals. It will give way under the weight of a human, causing them to fall through to the floor below, a fall of 3 metres.

The chamber below contains a weapon, dating back to the Time War. It's a Stasis Field Generator; a gun that freezes its target in time. It's got a limited area of effect, but can freeze everything within a few metres of a designated point. So, aim it at a bunch of soldiers, pull the trigger, and they're frozen forever. Well, as long as the weapon's batteries last or until it's fired again.

The weapon has already been fired, at an enemy of the time capsule's crew. The character who falls through the floor lands at the feet of whatever horrible monster your players hate the most: a Dalek, maybe, or a Weeping Angel. This monster is frozen in time and is perfectly harmless... so long as the players don't meddle with the Stasis Field Generator.

If they do use the Stasis Field Generator, though, to zap the Military Expedition or the Wolves, then they'll find themselves swapping one problem for another.

THE LIBRARY

If it weren't for the shelves lining the walls and free standing in rows in this area one might think it was another warehouse. However, the library has been appropriated as a Silverfish hive. Paper and card and binding materials now form the bedding for row upon row of little nests, each containing Silverfish eggs. Inside the eggs it's easy to see the movements of the bright and wriggling creatures. If one were to look around what has become a hatchery one might notice that many of the eggs are dead, the creatures within more yellowing than white, making spasmodic twitching motions, if they move at all. There are a number of Silverfish here as guardians of the young, and they will jump to attack any transgressors.

The library is a great opportunity to throw red herrings at the player group. It wouldn't be outside of the bounds of possibility to have a book here, barely recognisable but definitely from the native time period of the party themselves. How strange to have found a book on the life of Vincent Van Gogh in this strange decaying place on the edge of space!

THE MENAGERIE

This is a long hall that seems to be free of Silverfish and mostly free of Milk Mushrooms. It contains a number of glass cases, fogged and decayed, though close examination will reveal that these cases house (or housed) plastic models of alien races, some fantastic and some familiar. It might be disturbing to come across a glass case containing the face of a human being – half eaten away by time, the other half quite realistic – staring out at you.

It's important to note that there are no examples of Silverfish or Wolves in the glass cabinets here. All of the species modelled in the menagerie were put here by the previous inhabitants of the time capsule, back when it was an active time-and-space-going vessel.

THE SWIMMING POOL

The swimming pool has long since evaporated but the tiled remains as a testament to the fact that humanoids who lived here once enjoyed swimming.

There is what basically amounts to dry soil in the bottom of the pit, sterile and evil smelling.

The bottom of the pool has an intricate mosaic design that's mathematical in design but doesn't depict anything in particular. Not that most people are going to spend enough time down in the soil to discover this, or to excavate the whole thing if they did.

The automated plumbing to refill the pool still works – if the characters meddle with the controls, they may dump a few thousand gallons of water on top of themselves.

⚙ 5. THE WOLVES IN THE CONSOLE ROOM

Eventually, those exploring the core of Anomaly IV will find themselves heading down a staircase and into a large circular room. This is where things might start to get awfully familiar for the players, if not their characters.

The stairs end in metal gridding that forms a floor above an area of what looks like intricate and complex machinery, with cogs made of diamonds and emeralds that have ceased their motion but still glitter and sparkle whenever light catches them. In the middle of the room is a circular control panel built around some huge pillar of what looks like faintly glowing jade, tall enough to reach into the ceiling.

The control panel is insanely complicated with cogs, buttons, levers and small panels containing lights. If the characters have a TARDIS of their own, they will recognise it at once for what it once was: this ship's console room.

The central column of the room's light pulses gently: the very heart of the Anomaly and the cause of the dimensional disturbance. It is here that the Wolves sleep, basking in the eerie green light from the column, curled around each other and over each other, huddled together for warmth. The whole room has a musky smell, and the sound of their breathing is like the sound of an ocean at night.

This many Wolves in the same place at the same time could be very dangerous indeed, even for a group of well-armed, well-organised characters. Furthermore, there's no way of getting to the central console except through this enormous and perilous puppy pile.

If the characters are in the Scientific Expedition's dimension at this point in time they will see Professor Kelly-Hotel off to one side of the puppy pile. The Professor is to be food for the young Wolves but while they sleep he is held down by their bodies. The Professor is awake, deathly afraid and bleeding from several nasty wounds already. He is wiser than to make a move or shout to the characters; rather he looks at them pleadingly. In the case that there's any of his team with the characters they will immediately want to try to rescue the Professor. However, we've already established that the Scientific Expedition cannot withstand a full-scale attack from four or five Wolves; there is easily ten times that number here.

Lying off to one side of the young Wolves, not far from the Professor, is a larger specimen – the den mother. She is the de facto leader of the Wolves on the Anomaly, and also the mother of the young. She is obviously better fed than the Wolves that the party have seen so far, her fur jet black and her teeth unnervingly visible (her stats can be found on pg. 57).

If the characters are instead in the Military Expedition's dimension, this could be time for the soldiers to go to work. Unless the characters are armed and have shown themselves capable of using those arms they will be used in a tactical role only during such a battle, helping to put together a plan of attack and letting the soldiers implement it. And then the troops go to work, taking care of the Wolves. This isn't going to save the Professor, however.

Any attack on the sleeping Wolves by the characters on their own, or just backed up by the Scientific Expedition, is likely to end badly with the team and the characters forced to retreat (the Wolves are fighting for their territory here and will not follow a retreating foe).

The best solution is to borrow tactics and advanced weaponry from the Military Expedition, which will allow the scientists to be able to better combat the threat. It will also serve as a dry-run for what's to come: killing the TARDIS at the heart of Anomaly IV, which they will only be able to accomplish by using technology from both dimensions.

However, there are possible solutions other than violence. Most of the Wolves could be drawn away from the console room by a party that is loud and noisy enough to advertise their presence as an alternative (and more plentiful) food supply. However, it should be borne in mind that the Wolves know how to jump between the parallel universes, so relying on a convenient rift to carry them away from the console room and any pursuing Wolves will not work as well as they might expect. This option should turn into a long chase with the characters either having to hide to escape the Wolves or use their ingenuity to somehow trap their pursuers.

Either way, if the Wolves are lured away or trapped, the den mother should stay behind to guard the room and the Professor. The characters will have to face her sooner or later, even if they escape her children!

The Gamemaster should be lenient when it comes to inventive solutions as well – in the vastness of the Anomaly, with all those warehouses and storage rooms there is likely to be equipment which the characters might be able to use in order to overcome the wolves. If you've given your players a Skonnos blaster to play with, don't be surprised when they try and use it. Using the Stasis Field Generator here would be really unwise – who knows what happens if you try to freeze part of a TARDIS' console in time?

Once rescued, Professor Kelly-Hotel will need to be carried back to the Scientific Expedition's base of operations in order to be treated for wounds he has suffered. However, he has had some quiet time to think, and has performed some observations on the core of the Anomaly. He has already ascertained that there are rifts in space around the entire area and has a plan for detonating the core in order to put a stop to its effects on the surrounding space. However, the Scientific Expedition doesn't have an explosive charge hefty enough to do the job.

Any character examining the console will have trouble operating it (most of the controls are broken, and time capsule controls are isomorphic anyway – they will only work for the authorised operator.) However, anyone with any kind of experience with the TARDIS or time capsules in general will know what this is, and might be able to surmise what has happened in order to create the Anomaly from the body of a time capsule. If the party can't do this for themselves than it might be a good idea to spend a Story Point to figure it out, or enlist the aid of Kelly-Hotel in order to act as the boffin. Whichever way it happens, the cat should now be completely out of the bag, and the race should be on to destroy the time rotor at the heart of the Anomaly, thus killing the time capsule for good and fixing the hole in the universe.

Poking around inside the central console yields some important information in the form of a holographic recording of the original pilot's last words, recorded by the capsule itself:

The woman's face is streaked with something – blood, dirt, soot, maybe. It's hard to tell in the shimmering blue-coloured projection. Her regal-looking clothes are torn and battered like she has been through a fight. The look of desperation in her eyes is unmistakable. She looks at something out of view and winces. When her head turns back to look at you she's crying.

"This is it. This is the end. There's nothing I can do now, nowhere to go. I'm going to die and I can't even

regenerate to save myself. I'm setting a course for deep space – you know what to do, don't you? Find somewhere quiet. Overload your engines. After a thousand years they'll think you're just another asteroid. Goodbye, precious one... goodbye." Her fingers scrabble at the controls, playing over their surface, though the effort obviously costs her dearly. With a final exhalation she slumps, and the projection abruptly snaps off.

Make sure your characters see this message; it's their only real link to the reality of what the Anomaly is. If you don't think they're going to find it by themselves then there's no reason that the recording can't play automatically.

⚙ 6. TO KILL A TIME CAPSULE

By the time the characters get to this point in the adventure the console room in both dimensions should be free from Wolves. If Professor Kelly-Hotel has been rescued he will have recovered enough to talk and be able to advise them on the state of the Anomaly. Assuming everyone's on the same page regarding what's to be done, there are several issues that will need to be taken care of.

Firstly, neither expedition has all of the appropriate equipment to do it. The Scientific Expedition will immediately point out that they don't have the necessary explosives to destroy the core. Of course, the Military Expedition do, and they should be open to persuasion to give something to the characters for the purpose, although this should raise the second

big question: what happens to the two expeditions when the explosion goes off? Considering the two expeditions are the result of the dimensional rifts, will they both die, be combined in some way or simply cease to exist? This might be a talking point or bone of contention for some parties; given that all of space is endangered by the Anomaly should they consider the fate of the expeditions or just allow the universe to sort itself out?

The expeditions themselves will have their own views on the matter: the scientists will be happy to see themselves sacrificed in the name of making the universe safe, the soldiers markedly less so, unless it is pointed out to them that the destruction of the Anomaly could end the war on Pilatedes by proving that the Anomaly is just an astronomical oddity rather than anything supernatural or mystical. All of the soldiers would die to see an end to the conflict after all.

The truth of the matter is that with the Anomaly destroyed, there will be one Pilatedes with one Quorum. What that looks like in the wake of the destruction is left entirely up to the individual Gamemaster and is beyond the scope of this scenario. It should be shaped, however, by the actions of the players, and the universe they choose to be located in when the Anomaly is destroyed.

A combat-hungry party may also have a final battle against Wolves to contend with. Whatever Wolves were not killed earlier will attack anyone in the console room while the characters are planting charges there.

There is also the small matter of getting everyone out of the Anomaly, and this should be the final part of the adventure – setting the explosives and then having both expeditions as well as the characters themselves run back to their respective ships to escape before the Anomaly is destroyed. A Gamemaster who wants to inject some more tension into this last mad dash could easily have the way back blocked by some of the last surviving Wolves, or alternatively have the way back run through a warehouse that forms the home for a colony of Silverfish so that the characters have to trudge through Milk Mushroom debris, hatched egg casings and kick out at wriggling and writhing bodies.

From the perspective of outside the Anomaly, the characters should be able to see just one escaping Quorum spacecraft – they will either be in one dimension or the other. The explosion the characters caused will not be visible. However, once it has

occurred, the Anomaly will slowly implode: the vast and unruly collection of rooms and stores on the outside of the structure collapsing in until there's nothing left but one circular room.

Finally, that last room warps space, shrinking impossibly until it folds up through itself and vanishes into nothingness. If possible, a message will be sent to the characters to say that the expedition is fine. Those aboard will be safe and sound, and the surviving expedition will be native to whichever dimension the player party was in when it left the Anomaly. Essentially, the players will have made the final decision as to who survives and who is simply brushed under the rug that is the grand scheme of the universe.

⚙ AFTERMATH

So, the Anomaly was destroyed, the time capsule at its core killed and the planet Pilatedes returned to being a single planet in a single dimension. A number of questions still remain, however:

- If this was designated Anomaly IV, what mysteries do the other Anomalies hold? What are they and where are they?
- What happened to the expeditions? What is the Quorum now, in this newly recombined universe?
- The Time Lords are gone, trapped away in their own parallel pocket dimension. Is there anyone who should be told of the final fate of the time capsule? Are there any consequences for the characters who have essentially killed it?
- Who was the original pilot of this time capsule? What caused her death and why could she not regenerate?
- What happened to the humanoids that originally brought the Wolves to Anomaly IV?

These are all questions for another adventure, perhaps, and are left for the Gamemaster to answer.

THE TOMB OF CLEOPATRA

THE TOMB OF CLEOPATRA

This story takes a group of characters back in time, to Egypt just after the Roman invasion. A conspiracy against the invaders, and a golden mask, hide traces of a returning foe.

On the asteroid base of Demon's Run the Doctor dealt the mysterious Order of the Headless a dolorous blow. But he did not defeat them all, and the Monks are nothing if not patient. The survivors of the order have set a trap for the Time Lord in Ancient Egypt, using salvaged pieces from the Twelfth Cyberfleet to give the impression that a Cyber-ship has crashed in Earth's past. The Headless Monks are impersonating the Cybermen because they want to play on the Doctor's character flaws; they want him to enter their lair overconfident and prepared for the wrong foe. The Headless Monks believe the Doctor won't take the time to investigate too deeply if lives are on the line.

Are the Monks right or are they wrong? Well, that really rather depends on your players, doesn't it?

⚙ ADVENTURE SYNOPSIS

The Tomb of Cleopatra can be played by groups of any composition. Some plot elements assume that the incidents in **A Good Man Goes to War** (see **The Eleventh Doctor Sourcebook**) occurred in your game's setting, but options are provided for groups where this isn't true (see the box out opposite).

The characters hear about an archaeological dig in the present day that has discovered the fabled Tomb of Cleopatra, but one of the artefacts recovered is an artistic representation of a Cyberman's head. The characters speak with the archaeologists before travelling back to Roman Egypt. Suspicion initially falls on a clerk named Sinhue, but he's not working for the Cybermen. The characters then trace the helmet to a group of slavers who are wearing bits of Cybermen armour. They trade slaves for this miraculous armour at a desert temple with a man who is completely encased in it. When the characters investigate, they uncover the true villain – the Headless Monks – but are captured and sentenced to death. The characters must escape and defeat the Headless Monks by destroying their time machine, sending them back to their own time.

It isn't vital that the characters follow this sequence: at each stage suggestions are given to take into account groups who diverge from the main plot.

⚙ ROMAN EGYPT

In 30 BC, Cleopatra VII, the last Queen of Egypt, was captured by the Roman general Octavian. He wished to take her to Rome in chains, for a procession through the streets followed by a public execution. Allies in the Royal Palace of Alexandria were able to hide a snake in a bowl of figs, allowing Cleopatra to commit suicide. Cleopatra's son, Caesarion, has been

WHAT IF THE BATTLE FOR DEMON'S RUN HASN'T HAPPENED IN OUR GAME?

There are several ways to adjust the adventure for groups who haven't played through the events of **A Good Man Goes to War**, or who don't have the Doctor in their group:

- The ruse is really true: swap out the Monks for a smaller number of Cybermen. The piece of equipment the characters sabotage at the end of the story is a transmitter that keeps the emotions of the Cybermen suppressed. If it is destroyed, they all die.
- The Monks set the trap for the Doctor, but it's the characters who get caught in it instead.
- Choose a recurring villain from the group's own past, and put them into the story, either using the ruse or else recruiting an army of controlled Cybermen.
- Perhaps the Headless Monks are trapped in the past. They have lured the characters there to steal the Artron energy from time travellers to escape. This allows the story to end in negotiation, if the players offer to rescue the Monks.
- Assume the trap is for the characters instead. In their personal future, they will harm the Order of the Headless terribly. These Monks are seeking revenge, or are trying to destroy the characters pre-emptively.

captured and his execution is imminent. Caesarion, is the actual son of Julius Caesar, while Octavian is Caesar's adoptive son: two heirs is one too many.

The capital of Egypt is the port city of Alexandria. The exact layout of the city doesn't matter to this story. While describing it, Gamemasters should remember that Alexandria is a meeting place for merchants and goods from all over Europe, Africa and the Middle East. Buildings are monumental and opulent. The lighthouse overlooking the harbour, by way of example, is a Wonder of the World and contains a mirror made of Chinese iron. People from Alexandria like to think they have seen everything; they aren't shocked by strange manners, odd clothes or even apparently magical powers.

The clerk who smuggled the snake to Cleopatra is called Sinhue. He pretends to serve the Romans, and is now lowly enough that he avoids notice. He is the leader of a resistance movement that uses treasures secreted in Cleopatra's time to follow her dying instructions. Sinhue also had Cleopatra's body stolen and buried, with full rites, in a place where the Romans could not find her. He is buying weapons and recruiting soldiers, in an attempt to liberate Caesarion, from the Palace. Sinhue's activities make him appear suspicious, but he's not a servant of the Monks.

A CRACK IN TIME

There's a complicating factor that characters who make an Awareness + Knowledge roll (Difficulty 9, +2 bonus if they have Feel the Turn of the Universe) uncover. Octavian's life is, in many respects, fixed in time. Much as it's impossible to assassinate Hitler, because his life is a fixed point, so too is it impossible to kill Octavian.

If Octavian doesn't become Augustus Caesar, first Emperor of the Romans, it will trigger a temporal paradox (at best). Nonetheless someone is trying, using methods involving time travel, and this has caused tiny cracks in the fabric of the universe as time-space begins to fracture. This revelation is best made to the characters after the first scene, for maximum dramatic impact.

⚙ 1. BAIT

The adventure begins when one of the characters sees a news article that says the Tomb of Cleopatra has been discovered – one of the great archaeological discoveries of the 21st century! Its treasures are to be unveiled to the world at a new exhibition, but one of the artefacts shown in the article is described as a "golden helmet with the Eyes of Horus". This is, however, clearly a gilded representation of a Cyberman's head – this should pique the characters' interest sufficiently to set them off to investigate.

At this point the characters have several options:

- They can charge off into the past, guided only by the news article and luck, in which case the story moves on to **Arrival in Alexandria**.
- They can invite themselves to the opening night of the exhibition. They might just buy tickets, like

EXAMINING THE HELMET OF HORUS

The amount of information the characters can gain from the Cyberman's head depends on how they examine it. Characters who just look at the helmet in a museum display or quickly scan it with a Gadget won't get nearly as much information as a character who is allowed to hold and scrutinise the helmet up close. Awareness + Craft rolls suit characters just looking at the helmet. Archaeologically minded characters might prefer to make Awareness + Knowledge or Awareness + Science rolls. Those using advanced equipment to scientifically test samples taken from the helmet can roll Awareness + Technology.

A character who successfully examines the helmet in the case can tell:

- Some sections of the helmet are held together with small rivets.
- These are not found on a real Cyberman (but the character must have seen a real Cyberman to realise the significance of this).
- The gold has been applied to the helmet as hammered leaf, not electroplated. This means it was created by a person with a hammer, not a modern machine.

A character who successfully examines the helmet up close can tell:

- It is functional as a mask. It could be worn by a person.
- It is made predominantly from leather, over a bone frame. This makes it lighter than expected, if the character imagines it to be solid gold.
- It has been sewn by a master-craftsman, using techniques that are correct for the discovery period.

A character who successfully takes scientific samples can tell:

- Carbon dates from the leather are roughly correct for the period. The bones come from cattle.
- The gold has been diluted with silver, and so is technically not gold, but electrum. The silver doesn't have much copper in it, which is what causes silver to tarnish. The silver has probably been added to make the mask's materials cheaper.
- It is possible to examine metals for trace elements to determine where they were mined. Any laboratory concludes that the silver comes from a known deposit in North Africa, but the gold comes from a source never recorded before in an archaeological database.

A character who successfully uses advanced technology (TL 6+) can tell:

- The gold came from a planet with a far heavier load of transuranic elements than Earth, and wasn't processed using contemporary human techniques.

normal people, although this makes accessing the archaeologists themselves more difficult, or they can come up with some sort of ruse (like using their Psychic Paper).

- They can also break into the museum, to ransack the notes of the archaeologists and purloin some artefacts. Groups who first make a legitimate visit find later, surreptitious visits easier, as they know the lay of the land, and may have stashed Gadgets inside the building.

THE FROCKING-UP VARIANT

Characters attending the exhibition's opening night need a ticket. They can either obtain one legitimately, or bluff their way past the staff on the door. If the characters have status, power or influential friends, they may be able to wrangle a ticket. Characters may, instead, just confuse or bribe the security team on the door (Presence + Convince, Difficulty 15).

The characters might steal a pass (Coordination + Subterfuge, Difficulty 12) or pose as waiters and waitresses, or use some clever trick like their Psychic Paper.

The evening opens with drinks and canapés, as guests are given time to be seen while they examine the exhibition, and hold some of the less important

artefacts. The museum's director then makes a small and obsequious speech. He introduces Dr Claire Reeves and Matthew Dale, who make brief presentations about their work.

The museum director then makes a further, slightly undignified, grab for some of the cash he sees floating around the room, before disappearing to pick his daughter up from cub scouts. The crowd then mingles, discussing the artefacts. The archaeologists each gather in a small, interested group to discuss their work. The other guests prefer to socialise with friends, and peter out with the refreshments.

DR CLAIRE REEVES

AWARENESS	2	PRESENCE	3
COORDINATION	3	RESOLVE	3
INGENUITY	4	STRENGTH	3

Dr Reeves is a skilled archaeologist who has discovered an unexpected royal tomb. She is in her sixties, and originally from Cornwall, although she now spends all the time she can afford in Egypt. Her hair and eyes are brown, and her face has the mass of freckles pale people develop when they work in the sun for decades. Dr Reeves is well thought of by her colleagues, but known to be driven and difficult to track down when she's on expedition. The tour of the relics is an example of her stubborn dedication to her work. Usually, a major site like the tomb would be kept quiet, and offered to someone else who had funding to continue the work. The tour, which is happening only with the grudging support of the Egyptian government, will allow Dr Reeves to finish the dig herself, if it is successful. Dr Reeves

would make a great companion in her own right – she'd certainly leap at the chance to see Ancient Egypt for herself.

SKILLS
Athletics 1, Convince 3, Craft 2, Knowledge (Egyptology 7) 5, Medicine 2, Science (Archaeology 6) 4, Survival 2, Technology 3, Transport 1.

TRAITS
Charming: Dr Reeves speaks with an infectious zeal, particularly about her work.
Obsessed (Minor Bad): Her work.
Resourceful Pockets: Actually a backpack filled with useful stuff.

EQUIPMENT: Backpack, basic survival and medical gear while on digs, durable notebook computer, camera, museum security pass.

TECH LEVEL: 5   **STORY POINTS:** 12

Either of the archaeologists can provide the location of the tomb, although they will be hesitant to do so, fearing the site will be raided, its walls defaced and its artefacts stolen. The senior archaeologist is Dr Claire Reeves. Dr Reeves is in her sixties, and is fascinated by what she has found.

Characters are likely to get more information out of her if they offer their interpretations of the items that she has yet to identify: roll Presence + Knowledge (Difficulty 18). If they are unable to get the location out of Dr Reeves, the characters might instead target her assistant, a postgraduate student called Matthew Dale. Matthew is nervous about his career after university, and is hoping to parley his involvement in this dig into work with a museum, archaeological magazine or television program. A Presence + Convince roll (Difficulty 12) or a suitably tantalising offer of future employment will get him to spill the beans.

The following information is freely provided by the archaeologists or gathered from the small white signs accompanying each artefact:

- The tomb was cut into a limestone cliff. It was the sort preferred by Ptolemaic court officials, not the opulent mausoleum that is mentioned in historical accounts.
- Many of the grave goods don't seem to be for Cleopatra at all, as they have other names upon them. Many royal burials, if rushed, reused material from older graves.
- Most graves have a biographical inscription in them, but this one has two: Cleopatra's and another one, written slightly above it, but defaced with a chisel. An Ingenuity + Knowledge or Science roll (Difficulty 12) will allow the defaced inscription to be read; it notes that the grave's original owner was a courtier named Sinhue, with experience in the military and the ear of the Queen. Sharing such a discovery with the archaeologists will instantly win their trust and approval.

THE COMFORTABLE SHOES VARIANT

The exhibition is open to the public, so the characters can simply buy a ticket. The sessions are sold out for the first three weeks. Characters not willing to wait patiently can find some scalped tickets online, bluff their way in past the museum staff using Presence + Convince (Difficulty 9) or use their handy time machine. The exhibition seems to be perpetually filled with primary school children on tours, but characters may still gather the freely available information on

the little signs (or via downloadable audio tour). There is also a short educational film of Dr Reeves, but it does not contain any useful information beyond identifying her as the excavation's leader.

The huge numbers of children in the museum are useful distractions for characters wanting to get a closer look at things, take samples, steal something or break into the staff areas of the museum. A character might set off a fire alarm or buy all of the chocolate bars in the vending machines and scatter them down the stairs. In either case, a stampede of schoolchildren grants time to perform some skulduggery with an Ingenuity + Subterfuge roll (Difficulty 6).

THE BALACLAVA VARIANT

The characters can gain access to the artefacts, and to the location of the tomb, by breaking into the museum. The easiest way to do this is to be allowed into the building by a security guard, cleaner or staff member who works nights (a restorer, for example). This can be done with bribery, bluff or force. Alternatively the characters can stage a heist, complete with zip lines from the roof and hacking into the archaeologists' computers. Roll Coordination + Transport or Subterfuge (Difficulty 9) then Ingenuity + Technology (Difficulty 12).

WE DON'T HAVE A TIME MACHINE!

It's perfectly possible that the characters might not actually have a means to time travel – they might be a UNIT squad, for example, or members of Torchwood. In this case, a tweak of the plot is required. Here are three suggestions:

- One of the other artefacts brought back from the tomb is actually a time machine that will send anyone nearby back to Alexandria. The characters get caught in the energy field projected by this trap. Later, they can find a way back using the Headless Monks' own time machine at the temple.

- The Doctor has already discovered the Headless Monks' plans, and decided to send someone else to deal with the danger while he foils the Monks elsewhere in time. He arranges this by placing a Vortex Manipulator among the artefacts in the museum, keyed to the energy signatures of the characters. Once they have sprung the trap, he arranges a way for them to get home.

- The characters may go into the past because of a predestination paradox. While talking to the archaeologists, they see a stela (ceremonial door) in the uncatalogued finds. It is marked with a symbol they find personally significant (a Torchwood or UNIT logo, for example). When they investigate the stela, they find a hollow that contains a small strip of gold into which an instruction has been scratched. It is signed by one of the characters. If they, for example "take the strange coil in locker 417 and slide it into the base of the stela" it opens a portal to Roman Egypt. The stela is a machine called the Chronal Engine. The Headless Monks used it to travel to Roman Egypt. If the characters follow the suggested course of play, they sabotage the Chronal Engine to force the Monks, and themselves, back to their original times. This leaves the characters, at the end of the story, with a working time machine, so all they need to do after coming home is leave themselves instructions on how to fix it, and have an ally in the past break it correctly and bury it in Cleopatra's tomb.

The Museum has multiple levels of security, requiring rolls against a variety of skills. Barriers might include moving nets of lasers (Coordination + Athletics to dodge past, Difficulty 18), pressure plates (Awareness + Athletics to avoid, Difficulty 12), electronic locks (Coordination +Technology to disable, Difficulty 18), depowered elevators (Strength + Athletics to lever the doors and climb the cables, Difficulty 15), cameras (Coordination + Subterfuge to avoid or Technology to disarm, Difficulty 18) and patrolling guards (Coordination + Subterfuge to avoid, either Strength + Fighting or Presence + Convince if met).

Once the characters have found the archaeologists' room, they can steal their laptops and work on them later, or break into them in situ. This is an Ingenuity + Technology roll (Difficulty 9). Matthew Dale's password is his girlfriend's name, so characters who have gently quizzed him for biographical information, who look him up on a popular social networking site or who spend a Story Point will find it easy to guess.

⚙ 2. ARRIVAL IN ALEXANDRIA

The characters arrive inside a small warehouse off the main market in this section of Alexandria. The characters should have a little time to wander the streets, shop for trinkets and, if he's with them, be impressed by the Doctor spouting random and dubious recollections about the people of the time.

Eventually they will hear a disturbance at the other end of the market. If they head toward it, a man runs past them and hides in a snack vendor's shop. He has a large knife strapped over his left shoulder. An Awareness + Knowledge or Science roll (Difficulty 9, +2 bonus if the character has the Feel the Turn of the Universe trait) will reveal that the knife is an object out of its own time.

An attempt on Octavian's life has failed, and the assassin has fled into the bustle of the market; the Romans have sealed the streets that exit it. The guards from the palace, supported by the legionaries who always garrison the market, start grabbing people whose clothing and build roughly match their quarry. The description they have is poor, and they want to present the people they capture to eyewitnesses. It is this, and the offended cries of the people of the market, that attracts the characters.

The Romans have been hassling the vendors, and some have responded by flinging bits of fruit or buckets of dregs at them. An Egyptian who does this might be flogged or beaten if caught, but it has been done before, and both sides expect it.

Play this for comedy value, and let the characters throw some fruit too if they wish. Before the characters can properly get involved, a Roman pushes over a vendor's table. A young man, wanting to impress the vendor's daughter, throws a stone at the legionary. The mood swiftly changes.

The characters can see the stone in the air. If they have some strange power – or really quick reflexes – they might be able to deflect it from its course. If they

do not manage it, the legionary stumbles forward, his hands covering his face, blood trickling out between his fingers. At this stage of history, antibiotics don't exist. Any wound that bleeds might become septic, then fatal. A man with an open wound who has been doused with a bucket of dung has good reason to worry.

These soldiers don't just laugh wounds to their tent-mates off. They draw their weapons, and begin cutting their way through the crowd. They are happy to pursue the assassin, the boy who threw the stone, anyone who threw dung at them or anyone they take a dislike to. The Egyptians flee in panic, and many are hurt by either the Romans or the crush, by falling objects, by fire from overturned braziers or by panicked livestock.

The characters need to deal with the Romans. They can flee, hide or can confront the soldiers – or come up with some clever plan of their own!

FIGHTING THE ROMANS

There are a couple of dozen Romans in the market, but there are also almost a hundred Egyptians. If the characters start a riot, they only need to deal with a few of the legionaries themselves.

ROMAN LEGIONARY

AWARENESS	3	PRESENCE	2
COORDINATION	3	RESOLVE	3
INGENUITY	2	STRENGTH	3

If you've seen a movie with Roman soldiers in it, imagine that. The legionaries prefer to form a shield wall, soften the crowd up with javelins, and then charge in with swords. If allowed to fight like this, add +2 armour, as the Romans protect each other. Characters fighting them have a better chance if they can split the formation.

SKILLS
Athletics 3, Convince 1, Craft 3, Fighting 4, Marksman 3, Subterfuge 2, Survival 1.

TRAITS
Code of Conduct: Roman military law is merciless on soldiers who breach it.
Tough

EQUIPMENT: Swords (2/5/7) and javelins (2/5/7). The Romans wear boiled leather armour with metal plates upon it (2).

TECH LEVEL: 2   STORY POINTS: 2

FOLLOWING THE FLEEING MAN
The would-be assassin, who is called Narmer, has hidden in a store off the market. He knows the Romans have sealed the exits from the market, so he's making an alternative escape route. The rear wall of the store is made of wattled sticks daubed with mud and whitewash. He's cutting a hole through the wall to climb out onto an unblocked street.

Narmer continues doing this while talking to the characters. Their responses are reported back to Sinhue, if Narmer escapes.

Narmer remarks that the characters speak perfect Egyptian. He tells them he is a freedom fighter. He is unwilling to give them the Knife of Semet, or let them examine it, because it may be the only weapon that can kill Octavian. He pleads with them, for the life of Caesarion the King, to let him go in peace. He doesn't have time to fight the characters and will flee if they will not let him go – handle his escape using the Chase rules. This shop deals in deep fried pastries, so Narmer might kick over the frying pots, so that the floor of the shop is covered in boiling oil, to aid his escape – this is a Stunt.

NARMER

AWARENESS	3	PRESENCE	2
COORDINATION	3	RESOLVE	3
INGENUITY	2	STRENGTH	3

SKILLS
Athletics 3, Convince 1, Craft 3, Fighting 3, Marksman 3, Subterfuge 3, Survival 2.

TRAITS
Quick Reflexes
Tough

EQUIPMENT: Knife (2/5/7).

TECH LEVEL: 2   STORY POINTS: 2

TALKING THE ROMANS DOWN
A character can draw the attention of the officers of the Romans, and then convince them to stop the attack. This requires a Presence + Convince roll (Difficulty 12). This is simpler if the character can present a credible method for the assassin's escape, for example the hole in the snack vendor's wall. (Difficulty 9).

AFTER THE ROMANS LEAVE
Following the riot, the marketplace is wrecked and full of injured people. The characters can act freely here, doing anything from triage to filling their pockets with unguarded antiquities. Whatever they do will be observed and widely reported. NPCs, whose aid the characters may later seek, will take note.

THE KNIFE OF SEMET

Narmer is carrying a weapon that he thinks is magical, called the Knife of Semet. It was used, so stories say, by an ancient hero to kill a vast river monster that may have been a godling. The Pharaohs thought they were godlings, and stored it carefully in their royal armoury, partially to keep themselves safe, and partially to have a weapon handy to kill immortal relatives with. Sinhue stole the knife, as he had heard Octavian was a demigod and immune to mortal weapons. In truth, Octavian's a mortal man, but his life *is* fixed in time. Usually Sinhue's efforts wouldn't be able to damage the time-stream; they'd simply fail, but his knife is exceptional.

The Knife of Semet is thought to be made from "sky iron", like all early Egyptian iron objects. That is, the locals think it is made from melted-down meteorites. They're not far wrong; it's actually made from a shard of the hull of a Sontaran battle cruiser. Characters can determine that's it's not from Earth with an Awareness + Knowledge roll (Difficulty 9, +2 bonus on the roll if they possess Feel the Turn of the Universe, or are themselves a Sontaran). The blade is made of dull blue metal, with no sign of rust or chipping, and so it looks odd even to unskilled people.

The time travel method the Headless Monks are using is primitive: it can only take them back to places where the timeline has already been disturbed. To make time travel easier, they have corrupted the timeline by using a flaw in time to travel very early in Earth's history, then scattering about objects from the future. These, in turn, further abrade time when they hit fixed events, allowing the Headless Monks to access new points of temporal weakness.

The Knife of Semet is one such object. It is capable of making time crack, ever so slightly, when it is used to do things that shouldn't be possible. If the characters destroy the Knife, so that the possibility it will be used to assassinate Octavian entirely vanishes, then the cracks in time naturally close. This banishes the Headless Monks from this point in time.

If it seems that the destruction of the Knife by the characters will end the scenario prematurely, then the cracks in time only heal when the Knife is completely removed from Roman Egypt.

✴ 3. FINDING SINHUE

When the characters arrive in Roman Egypt, they are likely to pursue one of two leads: the Tomb of Cleopatra, or finding the courtier Sinhue. Finding the tomb eventually leads to a meeting with Sinhue.

FINDING THE TOMB

Trekking to the tomb is not difficult, if the characters already know its location. The tomb is in a barren valley, and there is no sign of excavation when the characters arrive. Sinhue's tomb was carved for him while he was young and serving in the army, so it was completed decades before he used it to bury Cleopatra and her grave goods in. One of Sinhue's followers is, however, watching the tomb, to make sure the Romans do not discover it.

If the characters find the tomb, Sinhue is made aware of their interest. One of his people tails the characters, since they do not appear to be either Romans or Egyptians. To spot their tail, the players may make an Awareness + Subterfuge roll opposed by the tail's Ingenuity + Subterfuge (which is 5) roll. If they attempt to interrogate their shadow, he flees. Sinhue assigns someone else, with better skills, to the same task. If the characters are seen to treat the Egyptians kindly or to oppose Roman authority figures, Sinhue sends a messenger to invite them to a meeting.

If the characters seem to be Roman spies, he has a group of his people kidnap the characters, trying not to harm them, so that they can be interrogated. At some point during this scene their food is drugged – the characters should make an Awareness + Subterfuge roll (Difficulty 15) to notice an odd smell or taste, in which case they can make an Ingenuity + Medicine roll (Difficulty 15) to identify the substance and whip up an antidote from random nearby supplies, before the drug takes effect. Characters captured in this way can escape, or they can convince Sinhue they are not Romans. See **Questioning Sinhue**, later.

BREAKING INTO THE TOMB

The tomb has three main rooms and several lesser chambers. The first room is easily accessed. It is simply defended by a ceremonial door fixed with a primitive lock, followed by a granite portcullis. The Gamemaster should pay close attention to how the characters break in, as how they circumvent a similar portcullis may be important later in the story. The room is a chapel. A statue of Cleopatra and an altar for offerings furnish the room, and the walls are decorated with painted scenes, displaying the life of a nobleman in paradise.

The other two rooms, which contain Cleopatra's treasures, are more difficult to reach. The corridor that leads to her body and treasures slopes down into the rock at a sharp angle. To seal it, Sinhue's workmen sealed the deeper end with a granite block, filled the passageway with a mixture of lime and sand, then pumped water into it to form a sort of cement.

If, somehow, they get past all that – and they'll have a tough time, unless they manage to use a Gadget to bypass all the cement – they'll find the tomb pretty much as the archaeologists eventually do back in the modern day. Just a little cleaner and less dusty. The Cyberman's head is present and correct, albeit about 2000 years newer. Much as it was in the modern day, it is a replica, not an original... but of what? The answer's not down here. They'll have to ask Sinhue.

FINDING SINHUE

Sinhue was a clerk and advisor in the Royal Household, but now that Cleopatra is dead, he has arranged employment in the vast grain warehouses by the docks. These are the source of Alexandria's

wealth, and are vital to the Roman army. This gives him political protection and provides him with cover while smuggling weapons. It's perfectly normal for new merchants in town to ask around for him, but he's leading a resistance cell, so he's both suspicious of others and acting suspiciously.

If the characters decide to put Sinhue under surveillance, they may make an Ingenuity + Subterfuge roll opposed by his Awareness + Subterfuge (which is 9) roll to observe his daily round of activities. The most suspicious thing they notice is that he is shipping heavy boxes into the city, and using his job at the docks to cover up his smuggling. The characters may also sneak into the great granary where he is storing these boxes using Coordination + Subterfuge (Difficulty 6 if they choose the right time of night, or higher at other times); if they succeed they'll find that the boxes contain stockpiled weapons.

QUESTIONING SINHUE

Earning Sinhue's trust, sufficient at least for him to tell them where the helmet came from, is not difficult, since it does not risk any of his collaborators in the planned uprising. It requires a Presence + Convince roll, with the the Difficulty depending on what the characters have done while observed:

- (Difficulty 6) The characters helped Narmer escape.
- (Difficulty 9) The characters have aided the Egyptians against the Romans, or they know about the tomb or weapons, but have not revealed them.
- (Difficulty 12) The characters have done neither harm nor good.
- (Difficulty 15) The characters have aided the Romans, but only in minor ways.
- (Difficulty 18) The characters led the Romans to the Tomb, the weapons or the assassin.

THE TOMB OF CLEOPATRA

SINHUE

AWARENESS	3	PRESENCE	3
COORDINATION	2	RESOLVE	4
INGENUITY	4	STRENGTH	2

Sinhue is a Greek Egyptian in his late forties. He dresses to appear older, stoops and dyes his hair grey. He is considered elderly for this era and he exacerbates this because Roman soldiers, particularly, tend to think that old people are idiots. He dresses like a wealthy courtier and carries a small knife up his sleeve.

Sinhue served in the army when he was a young man, and retired to the court after his first campaign. Before Cleopatra's death, he was her counsellor and messenger. Following her death, his personal goal was to see her properly buried, then avenged.

SKILLS

Athletics 1, Convince 4, Craft 2, Fighting 3, Knowledge (Ancient Egypt 5) 3, Medicine 1, Subterfuge (Spying 6) 4 , Survival 2.

TRAITS

Adversary (Minor Bad): The Romans know that there is a resistance leader, but don't know it is Sinhue.
Brave: +2 to resist fear.
Dark Secret: Leader of resistance cell.
Face in the Crowd
Friends (Major Good): Effectively he has a small army of fanatics, and the weapons and supplies to support them.
Obsession: Devoted to fulfilling his Queen's final wishes.

EQUIPMENT: Money, rich clothes, dagger (2/5/7).

TECH LEVEL: 2   STORY POINTS: 12

Sinhue buried Cleopatra in a tomb which he had prepared for himself, when he was younger and serving in the army. Some of the grave goods were his own, but because he could not inconspicuously order burial furniture in the market, and time was short, he paid criminals who rob tombs to provide him the extra items required. The Golden Mask of Horus was provided by one of these black marketeers. He arranges an introduction.

Sinhue can be convinced to give the Knife of Semet to the characters relatively simply, if they are honest with him. As an educated Egyptian, Sinhue believes the world is governed by mercurial gods and implacable destiny, which even they cannot ignore. Since the death of his Queen and her presumable ascension, he's been expecting a sign. If the characters say they are people with secret knowledge (time travellers, wizards, priests, oracles, madmen), that Octavian has a destiny, and that Sinhue is letting demons into the world by opposing it, that seems entirely plausible to him – at least it is if they can make a Presence + Convince roll (Difficulty 9).

Sinhue isn't gullible, however. The characters must prove they are the sort of people who know the workings of destiny. They can do this by performing a trick that would appear miraculous to a person from Ancient History. Medicine, the workings of the world and magic are all tied together in Sinhue's religion, so a wide variety of skills are appropriate. If the characters convince Sinhue to abandon his attempts at assassinating Octavian, he switches his attention to getting Caesarion to safety.

WHAT IF WE MISS BOTH CLUES?

If the characters did not find either the location of the tomb, nor work out Sinhue's name from the crossed-out inscription, then spending a Story Point will let them work out who stocked the tomb. It was presumably whomever stole Cleopatra's body from the Romans. The Romans can't discover Sinhue's identity because they face a wall of silence, but the characters at least speak Egyptian, which is enough for them to stumble Sinhue's way.

⚙ 4. THE TOMB ROBBERS AND THE BAZAAR

Sinhue's black market contact, Azione, has a store just off the bazaar where she sells linen clothing as cover for her family's grave-robbing business. Azione will not stand to be threatened for information; she has a dozen sons, grandsons and sons-in-law who work in the bazaar, all with weapons close to hand, and ready to come to her defence. Instead the characters will have to ask nicely.

If they ask about the origin of the grave goods she sells in general, or the Golden Mask of Horus specifically, then Azione is initially unwilling to give the names of her contacts. Azione will instead parley her information for some service or task they can offer – take a look at their character sheets and work out something they might be able to offer her. For example, if one of the characters has the Medicine skill, Azione has a sick grandniece that none of the healers can aid. If a companion has the Subterfuge skill, perhaps she wants their help to rob a tomb, so that they are as culpable as she is. Your players might even suggest their own tasks they can help with!

Once they have completed their allotted tasks, Azione will give them the name of a crafter – Okpara. Whenever Azione is paid in gold coins, or her boys find gold fragments when robbing a tomb, they take them to Okpara. He reworks their gold, and as much silver as he can manage, into impressive-looking, but fake, antiquities. She sells these to foreign merchants for far more than the dubious metal is worth.

Okpara told Azione that he had been paid to make the helmet by the leader of a band of slavers who come to the markets each month for new cargo. When Sinhue was looking for artefacts in a hurry, Okpara realised he had time to make a second helmet, so took the extra sale. Azione gathers that the slavers stay at a particular caravanserai when they come north.

THE CARAVANSERAI
Think of a caravanserai as a camping ground for merchants just outside the town. Huge tents, lots of animals and gear. People paranoid about thievery. Some trading, a lot of date wine. Many fights. Annoyed Roman soldiers watching on.

The eight slavers are led by a Roman called Gaius. They want to avoid the notice of the governing forces, because they were supporters of Mark Antony, who was allied to Cleopatra against Octavian. To avoid the possibility of being recognised by any of the Roman soldiers, they always attend the markets wearing Cybermen's helmets. They have convinced the locals that this is part of the religious customs of their desert tribe. Gaius has had made a gold Cyberman's helmet, so that he can look suitably chief-like. Each slaver also has a breastplate and gauntlets made from converted Cyber-ware, but they avoid wearing them unless they expect trouble; Egypt's too hot for metal armour, really.

The slavers always behave the same way while at the caravanserai, and other merchants are glad to gossip about them with a simple Presence + Convince roll (Difficulty 6). Two nights before they purchase slaves the slavers always carouse as hard as they can, so that they have a day to sober up before heading back down the Nile. They prefer to buy slaves in groups of 40, because each can handle a chain of five slaves. The slaves they buy are older, unskilled people, who sell for lower prices. If they are short on their quota, they kidnap drunks.

CONFRONTING THE SLAVERS
The slavers won't discuss their business: they don't want other traders muscling in on such a valuable trade route. If the characters want information, they'll need to separate a slaver from the group and crack him. Most methods of snatching a slaver require the characters to enter their camp. Some other suggestions are provided below.

- Convince Okpara to allow them to deliver the golden helmet to the slaver leader personally, with a Presence + Convince roll (Difficulty 12).
- As the players might have found to their cost, Sinhue has access to drugs that knock people out. Slipping some into their date wine requires an excuse to be in their camp, and a Coordination + Subterfuge roll (Difficulty 9).
- If the slavers don't have enough merchandise, they grab drunkards wandering home. The characters can lure a slaver into an ambush using Strength + Fighting, or another skill depending on the exact nature of the trap.
- The characters might release the slaves and use the ensuing confusion to grab a slaver. The slaves are kept on barges in the river, and a Coordination + Subterfuge roll (Difficulty 15) lets the characters sneak past the handful of guards on the barges and let the slaves loose.
- Sneaking into the camp, waiting for the slavers to fall asleep, and then gagging one, wrapping him in a carpet, and carrying him off. Roll Strength + Subterfuge (Difficulty 12).

THE SLAVER'S STORY
Once a slaver has been captured, he can be threatened or bribed into giving information:

- The slavers sell their victims at the Temple of Semet, to a strange man clad completely in steel armour, even in the middle of the day. His voice sounds oddly monotone.
- This Steel Man rarely rejects slaves, but they have been told that children, the insane or those with an illness are unacceptable.

- The slaves are paid for with thick gold thread, spun around pieces of iron, although they have sometimes bartered for pieces of the Steel Man's armour instead. Characters who investigate the gold thread may make an Ingenuity + Craft roll (Difficulty 9) to discover that it is wire, and is very pure. Similar wire is used by many civilisations in advanced electronics — but not in this age.

The characters' senses should be screaming out to them now that this sounds like a living Cyberman, loose in Ancient Egypt.

SLAVER

AWARENESS	3	PRESENCE	2
COORDINATION	3	RESOLVE	3
INGENUITY	2	STRENGTH	3

These deserters from the Roman army are mostly young men from Greece and Syria. They still have Roman weapons, and work with the precision of a small, trained unit. They lack discipline when not in combat, and most can be tempted to stupor with free wine. These characters believe they are members of a fundamentally superior group (the Romans) and see everyone else as potential merchandise. They see no reason to keep this opinion to themselves.

SKILLS
Athletics 3, Convince 1, Craft 2, Fighting 3, Marksman 2, Subterfuge 2, Survival 3, Transport 2.

TRAITS
Arrogant
Dark Secret: The slavers are actually all deserters and will be put to death if caught by Romans.
Distinctive: Those weird helmets kinda make them stand out.
Tough

EQUIPMENT: Swords (2/5/7) and various thrown weapons (2 /5 /7). The slavers' unique armour gives them 2 points of protection, but they tend to avoid using it except when in the city because it is so uncomfortable in Egypt's climate.

TECH LEVEL: 2   STORY POINTS: 2

OPTIONAL SCENE: SINHUE TRIES TO KILL OCTAVIAN

If the characters fail to convince Sinhue to call off his attack on Octavian, they get lucky and time does not collapse. Instead, Octavian's guards capture and torture the would-be assassin, who gives Sinhue up to the authorities. The Romans have Sinhue quickly and quietly killed. Octavian then orders Caesarion poisoned, his physicians paid to say he died of an illness. Octavian then reminds everyone that Egypt is his, gives his soldiers a large bonus and begins planning to return to Rome to fulfil his destiny.

⚙ 5. CHECKING OUT THE TEMPLE OF SEMET

The characters may spy on the temple before rushing in. The temple is a large rectangular structure with a single entrance. This large set of ceremonial doors, which are left open, leads into a courtyard. Behind the courtyard, up a set of stairs, is another huge doorway into a roofed building. The roofs indicate this building is divided into three sections. Facing the river is a tunnel, defended by a series of granite portcullises, which lets water into the building.

The temple courtyard displays several strange features. The strangest is the Cyberman seated on a stone throne, his back to the building's entrance, facing out of the courtyard. Two metal pillars stand at the top of the steps that glow with a gentle, artificial light.

Characters able to detect such things (Awareness + Technology, Difficulty 12) realise that the pillars are similar to an airport scanning machine. Using this device, whoever controls it can scan the health of any who pass between the pillars. Characters who succeed with a Fantastic success can also discern that the pylons are also set to detect residual Artron energy.

THE TOMB OF CLEOPATRA

CYBER-PUPPET

AWARENESS	3	PRESENCE	2
COORDINATION	3	RESOLVE	1
INGENUITY	1	STRENGTH	7

The Cyber-puppet is actually an advanced robot, encased in the shell of a dead Cyberman. The Cyber-puppet is faster than a true Cyberman and lacks their vulnerabilities. The Cyber-puppet has one additional quirk that may tell the characters that something is amiss. Real Cybermen have a tendency to utter the word "delete". The Cyber-puppet's controllers, when speaking with humans they believe Egyptian, use translation software to render their words, spoken through the puppet, understandable. When the TARDIS translator, or whatever other gizmo allows your characters to speak the local language, renders what the Cyber-puppet says back into their own tongue, the word the characters hear instead is "deface".

SKILLS
Athletics 3, Convince 0*, Fighting 4, Marksman 2.

* A Headless Monk speaking through the Cyber-puppet may use its own Convince score.

TRAITS
Armor (10): The working parts of the Cyber-puppet are jacketed in a shell made from mostly intact Cyber-armour. In the Cyber-puppet, the space usually reserved for machines that maintain the Cyberman's brain, and provide independent power, is instead dedicated to additional microservos, which enhance movement and compensate for the weight of the armour.

Dependency: The Cyber-puppet requires an external power source, provided in this case by an inductor in its throne. It remains seated because the Headless Monks have not been able to provide it with sufficient power to act independently for long. For every round spent free of the throne, it must spend a Story Point to do more than walk about or talk – as the Cyber-puppet does not have any Story Points of its own, its Headless Monk controllers will have to use their own Story Points.

Fear Factor (2): The Cyber-puppet might not have the presence of a regular Cyberman, but it looks identical to one so is still frightening..

Natural Weapon – Electric Grip: The Cyber-puppet's grip delivers a powerful blast of electricity It is, however, less lethal than a true Cyberman's grip, so only inflicts Stun damage.

Natural Weapon (Particle Beam): The arm-mounted particle beam looks genuine, but isn't quite as deadly as a Cyberman's inflicting (4/8/L) levels of damage.

Networked: The Cyber-puppet is capable of following preprogrammed instructions, but much of the time its movements and speech are controlled directly by a Headless Monk using a wireless signal.

Robot

TECH LEVEL: 6   STORY POINTS: 0

HACKING THE CYBER-PUPPET

One downside to being controlled remotely is that the Cyber-puppet's control signal can be hacked. The hard way to do this is to immobilise it and to crack open its casing and fiddle about inside. A much easier way to do this is to realise that the Cyber-puppet is actually a robot, detect the wireless signal used to control it and then use that as the avenue of attack. To do this, the characters need to block the signal and substitute it for their own. This will require an Ingenuity + Technology roll (Difficulty 18) and if successful lets them control it freely. The characters might also think to copy the Cyber-puppet's standby signal ("Scanning, No Threat Detected, On Standby") and keep broadcasting it (Ingenuity + Technology, Difficulty 9), in which case the Headless Monks will not detect their hacks, even if the characters' attempts fail.

ENTERING THE TEMPLE

The characters have several options to get into the temple without being detected. However, remember that the Headless Monks want them to break in and fall into their trap – they just need to put up enough resistance to make it look like it's not a trap.

Sneak over the walls. The temple has an anachronistic, futuristic modern alarm system. An Awareness + Subterfuge roll (Difficulty 15) is needed to spot and disarm it.

Pretend to be the mercenaries. If the characters simply march in, they are told to take their slaves to the cells, and then follow the glowing line on the floor to the treasury for their gold. If the characters lock the slaves into the cells, they notice that the cells have modern locks hidden within the wooden doors. They may also realise that there dozens of slaves here already, locked away - but not converted into Cybermen.

On the way to the treasury they pass through three vast, decorated halls. The roof of each hall is apparently held up by eight pillars. These pillars are really thin cylinders of plaster, with a Headless Monk hiding inside – because of their Flatline ability (see below), they will not register on any scans of the hall.

Once the characters are deep enough inside the temple, the Headless Monks burst from the columns and surround them. The Headless Monks demand their surrender, and threatening to kill the slaves if they do not.

Pretend to be slaves. If the characters allow themselves to be locked up instead, then they find surprisingly modern locks holding the cells shut. They may attempt to pick the locks with a Coordination + Subterfuge roll (Difficulty 18) but will have to be quick or else they'll be knocked out by gas released from vents hidden in the ceiling. If they manage to escape, they will be surrounded by monks, as above.

Break in via the water tunnel, then they come out in the Nilometer room. Metal shutters snap across the exit tunnel, and the Headless Monks demand the surrender of the characters, as described in the next section.

HOW DO THE HEADLESS MONKS TALK?

The Headless Monks talk to the characters using the Cyber-puppet, a speaker in the ceiling or through a head they carry around in a box. They do not open the box, but a creepy voice emanates from within it all the same.

✸ 6. THE TRAP AND THE ESCAPE

The Nilometer is the Headless Monks' chosen method of execution for the characters, for it is particularly suited for killing – properly killing, too – a Time Lord. A Nilometer is a deep, stone-lined well, but it has a marble column rising through its centre, with depths marked upon it.

Local people only owe taxes if the Nile's annual flood reaches a level suitable for agriculture, so this room was built be the temple's founders to see if they could collect taxes. The Nilometer links to the river through a large pipe, wide enough for a person to swim through, which is barred with a series of granite portcullises.

The Headless Monks want to drown the Doctor in the Nilometer because they know that a dying – or more correctly, a *regenerating* – Time Lord releases incredible amounts of energy, which could be dangerous or damage their equipment. The water, they hope, will absorb at least some of the heat generated when the Doctor dies repeatedly. The Headless Monks are not certain that this precaution is adequate, and so only a small number remain to watch the Doctor die. The Gamemaster should adjust how many depending on the make-up of the group. If the characters can defeat several Headless Monks, give the players that opportunity. If the players usually use guile to avoid violence, a single Headless Monk will suffice.

If the group has no Time Lord, the Headless Monks will still try to drown the characters in the Nilometer, but the Headless Monks have filled the Nilometer with deuterium oxide (heavy water) instead. Soaking the characters in this substance allows their machines to suck out the Artron energy stored in the bodies of time travellers. That the characters drown and are then eaten by Monastic Skulls is just an aesthetic bonus. Contact with heavy water is not dangerous: even drinking it won't harm the characters.

The Headless Monks force the characters to tie themselves, using linen ropes, to large stones through which holes have been drilled. These are ship anchors. While this occurs, the Head in the Box takes the opportunity to tell the characters – especially the Doctor, if he's present – how dreadfully predictable they are. In this exchange of jibes the Gamemaster may place a hook that leads to the next scene.

For example the Monk might mock them for being defeated by "A pile of scrap and a makeshift Artron Engine". The Gamemaster should lay the ridicule on thickly if the players are planning to reveal they are really in control of the situation at this point.

The characters then either jump, are thrown or have their anchors kicked into the Nilometer, and must escape. Use the Drowning rules from the ***Doctor Who Roleplaying Game***.

HEADLESS MONKS

AWARENESS	3	PRESENCE	5
COORDINATION	3	RESOLVE	4
INGENUITY	3	STRENGTH	3

SKILLS
Fighting 4, Knowledge 4, Marksman 5, Medicine 5, Subterfuge 4, Technology 3.

TRAITS
Alien
Alien Appearance (Minor): They're, quite literally, headless.
Code of Conduct (Major): The Order of the Headless are sworn to uphold the beliefs of the Church.
Dark Secret (Minor – Headless): Most people think their name is figurative.
Fear Factor 2: The Monks know they intimidate people and they never fail to take advantage of this. They spend most of their time completely silent (being headless and therefore mouthless helps with this), but at certain times they will begin to chant their prayers so everyone can hear. The sound of an army of Monks chanting attack prayers is enough to make anyone doubt themselves – if the Monks begin their keening attack song, their Fear Factor increases to 3.

Immunity (Fear, Persuasion)
Networked
Obligation (Major – Order of the Headless): Once you join the Order of the Headless, you join for life.
Psychic
Natural Weapon — Energy Blasts: The Monks combine ancient knowledge with futuristic technology, to good effect. They command a dangerous red energy and can summon it forth at will. It enhances the deadliness of their blades, and they can fire it out from their hands like a missile.
Special — Flatline: The Monks, despite being fully animated bodies, do not actually give off any life signs. They do not register as life forms to any standard scan.

EQUIPMENT: Sword 4/7/L; Energy Blast 3/6/9

TECH LEVEL: 7   STORY POINTS: 4-8

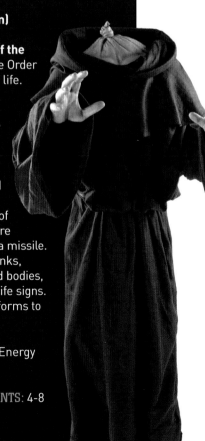

MONASTIC SKULLS

AWARENESS	2	PRESENCE	-
COORDINATION	1	RESOLVE	-
INGENUITY	-	STRENGTH	1

Monastic skulls, since they lack the ability to converse, are best represented as either animals, if dealt with in small groups, or as environmental effects, in large groups. The Headless Monks in this scenario use skulls only sparingly: intact skulls don't suit the Cyberman invasion ploy.

SKILLS
Fighting 2 (damage 1/3/4).

ESCAPING THE TRAP

The Headless Monks, as warriors who shun intellectual activity, have weaknesses that the characters can exploit to avoid death in the Nilometer:

- **They lack attention to detail:** The Monks don't know what the Sonic Screwdriver looks like, so discarding anything that is shaped like a wand satisfies them.

- **They are uncreative:** Having forced the Doctor to throw away the device that he is said to use to escape trouble, the Monks do not force him to empty his pockets. If characters can quickly create a gadget from the other items in the Doctor's pockets, while underwater, they may be able to use it save themselves.

- **They do not think his companions are significant:** Their war is against the Doctor, who is famous for crushing civilisations. The Headless Monks likely have no idea who the other characters are, and so do not care what abilities or equipment they have. They are just humans, and if they are thrown into a well, they are simply expected to die, not do remarkable things.

- **They are slightly gullible about conversion:** If a character asks to join the Headless Monks, his life will be preserved while one of them retrieves a box. This allows extra time to take the Headless Monks by surprise with some other plan.

- **They need to keep secrets:** If the characters can grab the Head in the Box, the Headless Monks are prepared to negotiate for its return, but only

if the characters threaten them with revealing its secrets. The Headless Monks don't care if, for example, the characters kill the Head in the Box. But the Headless Monks don't want the fact that they are literally headless to be proven to outsiders, nor do they want the method by which they create other Monks or preserve their heads to be detailed to their enemies.

- **They think they have controlled the Doctor's actions:** This is a perfect time for a gang of armed slaves, a hacked Cyber-puppet, the Roman army or Sinhue's resistance fighters to come crashing through the temple.

⚙ 7. FOILING THE MONKS' PLANS

If the characters escape the trap, the remaining Headless Monks gather together in a small room at the heart of the temple, where the Artron Engine is stored. They repurpose their generators to overload and explode, destroying the temple and anyone in it. As overload approaches, the noise becomes progressively louder and more highly pitched, and minor earth tremors of increasing violence occur. The characters will likely work out that something bad is getting inexorably nearer. This countdown gives the characters the chance to go on the offensive. If they force the Headless Monks to abandon their foothold in Roman Egypt, their equipment returns with them to the 51st century, preventing the explosion – or at least, shifting the explosion forwards in time to the Headless Monks' ship.

WHAT IS AN ARTRON ENGINE, ANYWAY?

An Artron Engine is a primitive time travel device. It looks like a stela (a ceremonial doorway), and its user steps through a temporal field generated within the frame to travel into the past. Artron Engines lack the capability to truly navigate time: they can only send things back to points where the time-steam is already damaged. Artron Engines contain a safety mechanism to retrieve travellers stuck in the past and prevent further damage of the timeline; if the device is ever switched off, the displaced beings slingshot back to their time of origin, leaving the device in the past, inert. A character with a suitable trait (such as Boffin, Feel the Turn of the Universe, Time Traveller or Vortex) or from Tech Level 8 or later may make an Ingenuity + Technology roll:

- (Difficulty 6) They know that the Artron Engine can only carry people to points where the time-stream is already damaged.

- (Difficulty 9) They know that the Artron Engine throws its users back to their original time if it is shut down.

- (Difficulty 12) They know that the Artron Engine can be shut down by destroying some of its components, or by removing the source of the damage to time.

The Artron Engine looks a bit like a stone door frame, but is actually a steel jacket filled with bits of technological wizardry. It can be separated into five parts, each about a metre long for transportation. Assembly and warm-up takes about 10 minutes. If the characters used the Artron Engine to travel to Roman Egypt (see page 81), they need to explain how it came to be in Cleopatra's tomb so as to close the destiny trap. The easiest explanation is that they put it there or had Sinhue place it in the tomb after they return home.

SWITCHING OFF THE ARTRON ENGINE
Access to the Inner Sanctum, where the Headless Monks have fortified their position, is easy, but the Headless Monks themselves are formidable opponents. Defeating them in combat, to reach the operator controls or simply to smash the obviously important bits, may suit some groups.

The players might come up with another plan though, such as using the floodgates to divert the Nile so that it washes through the temple.

They might devise a piece of Jiggery-Pokery to block the flow of Artron energy from the Time Vortex, switching the device off, or any number of other clever plans.

REMOVING THE TEMPORAL ANOMALY
The Artron Engine can only keep the Headless Monks in this period of time because there are small cracks in the time-stream. If the characters repair these, the Artron Engine loses its anchor point and the Headless Monks are dragged back through time to the 51st century. The cracks are being caused, inadvertently, by the use of Semet's Knife to attempt to assassinate Octavian. Once they've seen the Artron Engine and worked out what Semet's Knife really is, they can put two and two together with an Awareness + Knowledge roll (Difficulty 15, +2 on the roll if the character has Feel the Turn of the Universe). Destroying the knife, or throwing it back through the Artron Engine's portal or whisking it away in the TARDIS, all remove the temporal anomaly.

USING OCTAVIAN AS A SLEDGEHAMMER
The Headless Monks know that Octavian is a fixed point in time; he will become Emperor Augustus and start the Imperial era of Rome no matter what. If, therefore, the characters can somehow arrange for Octavian to personally attack the Headless Monks, they will be forced to retreat. Although they could hurt him, kill him even, they're not prepared to risk causing catastrophic damage to the time-stream.

⚙ AFTERMATH
Characters who have formed friendships with some of the NPCs might assist them in several ways, tying up the loose ends in the story, and find a satisfying conclusion.

SINHUE
Many of Sinhue's goals are literally impossible, given Octavian's destiny. He cannot kill Octavian, nor can he restore the Throne of Egypt to Caesarion. Sinhue can, however, save the young Pharaoh's life, provided that Caesarion disappears from history. Taking Caesarion in as a companion, perhaps, or even just taking him to a more comfortable part of the world – or beyond – allows Sinhue to put his duties to his Queen behind him, and seek a new life for himself.

There are folk-stories of one last Pharaoh who fled an invader, and founded a city either at a desert oasis or in the depths of the African jungle. These people were said to have kept Egyptian civilisation alive, carefully keeping themselves secret until Victorian times, using technological secrets lost to the rest of the world with the fall of the Library of Alexandria. The freed slaves, ruled by Caesarion, could be the kernel of these stories.

THE ARCHAEOLOGISTS
The Tomb of Cleopatra has not been thoroughly excavated yet, so items can be placed in the sections yet to be closely examined without changing the future. For example, a letter from Sinhue, on virtually any subject, would be a priceless artefact and advance the study of Egyptology to a degree not seen since the discovery of Tutankhamen. The characters could ask Sinhue to seal a letter in an airtight jar and hide it behind the wall plaster in a suitable section, marking the place so as to give the archaeologists a subtle hint. The Monks had scavenged about half a ton of gold wire from the Cyberfleet too. The player characters may use this to fund the excavation, or give it to the freed slaves.

INDEX

BBC
DOCTOR WHO
ADVENTURES IN TIME AND SPACE

THE DOCTOR WHO SOURCEBOOKS

Celebrating 50 years of Doctor Who, each Doctor Who Sourcebook takes a closer look at the adventures of one of the Doctor's incarnations. Each book has a detailed guide to every episode from that era, including information on the Doctor's allies, enemies, gadgets and aliens he encounters. It's not just a great resource for fans of the game, but for every fan of the show!

CB71105
ISBN: 978-1-907204-97-5
$34.99

CB71107
ISBN: 978-1-907204-98-2
$34.99

CB71112
ISBN: 978-0-85744-167-6
$34.99

CB71113
ISBN: 978-0-85744-176-8
$39.99

CB71114
ISBN: 978-0-85744-209-3
$34.99

CB71115
ISBN: 978-0-85744-216-1
$34.99

CB71116
ISBN: 978-0-85744-242-0
$34.99

CB71117
ISBN: 978-0-85744-248-2
$39.99

CB71118
ISBN: 978-0-85744-252-9
$34.99

www.cubicle7.co.uk